The information in this book reflects the ancient teachings, author's personal experiences and those of her clients and her expertise in the field of health and healing. I encourage you to use this book for self-healing. It is not intended, however, to replace professional medical care or treatment.

First paperback edition March 2022

Book cover design by Trish Campbell
Book back cover and layout design by
Trevor Stooke
Graphics by Trish Campbell

ISBN 978-1-7781151-0-3 (paperback)

ISBN 978-1-7781151-1-0 (ebook)

https://www.ayurvedichealingcenter.com

To be hopeful in bad times is not just foolishly romantic. It's based on the fact that human history is a history of cruelty and compassion, courage, sacrifice, and kindness. What we choose to emphasize in this complex history will determine our lives. If we see only the worst, it destroys our capacity to do something. If we remember those times and places – and there are so many – where people have behaved magnificently, this gives us the energy to act, and at least the possibility of sending this spinning top of a world in a different direction. And if we do act, in however small a way, we don't have to wait for some grand utopian future. The future is an infinite succession of presents, and to live now as we think human beings should live, in defiance of all that is bad around us, is itself a marvellous victory.

Howard Zin

Tribute to My Teacher, Cassandra

I would like to acknowledge and honour my teacher, Cassandra Tera Nova, who took me under her wings in the most trying time in my life and enlightened me with the metaphysical teachings that blew me away on one hand but resonated with me deeply as the truth. Her teachings connected the dots of my many lives which permeated my awareness to such a level that I see this life only as a continuum of the previous ones, making me feel a sense of wholeness in a way I had never known before.

So many of the teachings that I share in this book are what I learned from her. She truly is the embodiment of these teachings and no words can express my gratitude for her. You may find more information for her work here www.lightweavingjoy.com/cassandra.htm

Contents

Forward

Wake Up and Heal – 6 Steps to Emotional Freedom, holds great potential to heal the world.

I have written much about our remembering of our True nature and about taking personal responsibility for all we experience; in this life-changing book, Meena Puri has gone deeply into our abilities to awaken the Healer within. Puri and I are very much aligned on a Soul level and with the wisdom she shares in this book.

Meena Puri takes you on a deep inner journey so you can heal yourself.

She guides you to your inner spiritual warrior so you can heal from all past trauma, neutralizing the inner darkness in your own heart, reminding you of your own healing abilities. She guides you in finding the true liberation by connecting with the Source of your Being.

Mastering the Human condition through a process of deep exploration and self-discovery, she lays out a spiritual path that honors all of who we are. The ultimate freedom she speaks about comes from radical acceptance of what is and by being a conscious co-creator of the New Earth. In this way, we can all become the way showers through our own examples of self-healing and liberation.

We are the ones we have been waiting for!

Puri's book offers a clear pathway to healing the physical body through the highest spiritual lens of our true abilities. The physical body is the temple, and in part one of Puri's book, she defines what healing means - and that all disease is 100% energetic. "Our energy gets sick before our body does" as she says and to heal is to reconnect with Source.

In my book, "Peace – The Flip Side to Anger, How I used my emotions to heal my life and my body and HOW YOU CAN TOO", I talked about my own healing journey of how I healed myself using the principles Puri writes about in this book.

We are always in the process of "becoming" the truer version of ourselves and as Puri writes, we get to be the Truth tellers of the next generation. In this book, Puri reminds us that we are not our wounds, we are the extraordinary humans who can choose to transcend those wounds. Today's children will never experience those wounds because of our collective work to heal them.

Wake Up and Heal is an invitation for all of us to heal our body, mind and soul. You can hear Puri's soul calling in every word of her book; to activate the healing of this planet.

This book offers a practical approach to healing that anyone can use and practice. It is our choice, as Puri reminds us, to take the reins of our own well-being and co-create our Heaven on Earth. Heaven is nowhere but in our Higher States of Consciousness that we can cultivate through the technique shared in this book.

Kornelia Stephanie, Co-Creator of Heaven on Earth.

She is a champion of humanity's sovereignty, empowering all into authentic expression, inspiring self-healing, self-love, self-leadership, self-empowerment, and returning to the basics of co-creating the New Earth in harmony with Nature.

Kornelia is a well respected, leading-edge revolutionary for personal transformation and leadership. She is an Author, Metaphysical Teacher, Passionate Speaker, Powerful Master Coach, and Founder of The New House, The New Earth, the KS Media Group. www.korneliastephanie.com ~KS Media Group in the App Store

About This Book

This book is inspired by our current pandemic. We desperately need spiritual grounding and inspiration at this time. As a collective, we have witnessed and endured much darkness and pain in the last two years. The awareness of what we are collectively participating in creating is the bitter medicine that we need to wake up. What we see in the world is what we have created in some way, shape, or form. We can't deny our responsibility for what we are experiencing.

Feeling defeated at changing anything out there, we feel compelled to change what is in here. That's where it starts. It can't be any other way.

If we can recognize our inner power, listen to our inner wisdom and finally take the reins of our health back into our own hands, then the pandemic would have served its purpose.

Are you ready to free yourself from all past trauma? Are you ready to live from a place of deep connection and centeredness? Are you ready to uncover your True North and gifts? If you answered “yes” to one or all of this, then this book is for you.

The teachings I am about to share with you are profound in shifting you in ways that you never thought possible. I was guided to these teachings when I had thrown my hands in the air in utter frustration and emotional turmoil with my son. The teachings were like a balm to my wounds and I hope they would be for you as well.

I have organized the book into 3 parts.

Part I - What is healing

Part II - About energy

Part III - The 6 Steps: The 6A technique

First and foremost, I am a student. I am continuously evolving and growing, thanks to the many phenomenal teachers that I have encountered and continue to encounter. Being a practitioner of Yoga and Ayurveda, the teachings of Consciousness and Energy are at the heart of my being, and am drawn to the teachers who are aligned with the same. My work is currently greatly influenced by Dr. Joe Dispenza, Dr. Jean Houston, Dr. Christine Northrup, Dr. Paul Dugliss, and Esther Hicks, to name a few. This is a wonderful time in our history where we are merging Conventional and Holistic Medicine to reach the unfathomable heights in our health and human potentiality. These are incredible times indeed.

It's my sincere hope that this book serves not only as the starting point on your healing journey but remains your companion throughout.

From my heart to yours,

Meena Puri

Toronto, January 2022

The Ask of Our Times

"What incredible times we are living through", say the awakened ones!

"These are the worst times that I have ever experienced. I can no longer cope. When is it going to be over? When are we returning back to normal?", say the rest of us.

Let's lament over the lost "normal" if we must; the memories of which are fading away with each passing day. Seems like another lifetime, doesn't it?

It's seldom, if ever, we can turn back the clock. But do we want to, is the question.

Our lost "normal" was a time of overwhelm, overconsumption, over-busy, over-stressed yet we were happily (or so we thought) riding the hamster wheel in a quest for that good old Great American Dream. Only If we work harder, we could go on that expensive vacation or buy that big boat or whatever. In that "normal" we lost our health; we lost ourselves.

We didn't dare question and there seemed to be no time for it. Is there another way? What am I doing all this for? Am I happy? Whose life am I living? Do I just keep regurgitating the past experiences into my current life, in my relationships, in my health, in my work; all the meanwhile lying to myself that someday, I will slow down, someday I'll do what I really want to do yet secretly fearing that that day may never come?

That day, rather that time has come. It is NOW!

This is the time to slow down, to have a think, to ponder, to question, to reassess, to re-evaluate, to re-visit, to heal, and to connect to our heart's yearning.

We can choose either to wake up or stay asleep; waking up comes with a huge responsibility and staying asleep comes with a cost. There is no free lunch.

The choice is completely yours. What will you choose?

Waking up requires that we dare to ask ourselves some deep questions and allow the inner stirring to take place. What do you deeply desire? What do you deeply dare to express? What is your purpose in life? These are burdensome questions because they come with responsibility but the burden on our soul for not asking them is much greater. The truth is when we begin to ask ourselves these questions, we can no longer stay asleep and the good old “normal” may become less and less attractive. This is very unsettling to our ego.

We have been lulled into living an unquestioned life, seduced by the external glamour and glitter totally unaware of the programming and conditioning underneath. We dared not look into our inner world.

If you are still reading this, you are beginning to wake up. If you no longer can buy into your own bull shit, you are waking up. If the current status quo that you worked so hard in your life to maintain is making you feel uncomfortable, you are waking up.

When we begin to stir, it creates a ripple in all areas of our life. When it comes to our soul’s reckoning, everything is on the table.

What are we waking up to? What should we know? We are waking up to the Truth of who we are. I want to explain this as it has become a cliché in the spiritual world.

When I was teaching high school kids at the International Academy in Michigan, I asked them to write a paragraph about what their purpose was. I got interesting responses. Some wanted to save the environment, some wanted to go to Harvard, some wanted to get a high-paying job, some wanted to make lots of money to buy what they wanted, etc.

I asked them why they are studying in this hard school (IA is thought to be harder than the normal high school). "Because my parents wanted me to be in this school or so I could get into a good university." Why do you want to get into a good university? "So, I can get a high-paying job". So, what, I asked? I mean what will you do with all the money? "I'll buy a big house and maybe another home at the ski resort, I love skiing". So, what, I carried on. "I'll have kids, family, and vacations." So, what, I continued." Well, I guess I will die when I get old."

A deadly silence fell upon the whole class as this student said this out loud with a big question mark on his face; I am doing all this so at the end I just die?

That's how I introduced them to their soul and the evolution of their soul.

Our body will decay and so will our mind right along with it. Thank God!

What will remain is our soul. Our soul is the invisible, non-physical part of us that comes from God, Universe, Source, Consciousness. Our soul has information and supreme intelligence just like what it comes from. This is the Truth of who we are. We are each a soul, a tiny replica of the Universe, the part of us that does not die when we leave our body.

The growth of our soul does not return back to zero when we die, it stays at the level of its growth and evolution when we transition and continues to evolve with each lifetime.

Human life is a tool to evolve our soul. How we evolve is by being deeply in touch with our soul and living from our soul. When we do that, the Universal soul has our back; it supports us because it can live through us and come alive through us.

Now living a human life makes much more sense and it gives us a purpose.

It will serve us to nurture our soul. How do we serve our soul in our day-to-day living, in our relationships, in our education, in our jobs, in our social life? Simply asking this will lead you to the answer.

We have been given the gift of a pause, a bend in the road, to examine, to ponder, to seek, to look deep within, to get stirred, to change, to heal. This gift came at the cost of lost lives, great suffering, and despair and we are still paying. We can't afford to waste it. It's enough! We've suffered enough!

We don't need to butt our heads against the restrictions, there is a better use of our time. We are supposed to go where there are no restrictions. Our inner world, our creativity, our ability to dream and re-design our lives have no restrictions. We are supposed to go there during this time and remove the countless invisible masks we have been wearing for centuries.

We are at a crossroad, being caught between the temptation of the ego or the call of our soul. We are presented with a choice. We must understand the enormity of the choice and what’s at stake.

These times are asking that we *Wake Up and Heal*.

Part 1

What is Healing?

There lies a depth of wisdom, a boundless power, an array of possibilities, an undeniable yearning for life and freedom, an unshakeable trust and strength, an ocean of love, an untouched purity, and unclaimed peace. This is one universal truth that threads and binds all beings together. This truth escapes us as we put on the masks to stay safe, to stay untouched by life. The real journey before us is to peel away the masks that hide the treasure that we all already are.

Meena Puri

(quote from one of my articles in the local newspaper)

What is Healing?

Healing is a verb; a process, and healing is our journey of connecting to our soul. When we connect with that part of us, we become whole. Healing is our journey to wholeness.

According to Wikipedia, healing is the process of restoration from an unbalanced, diseased, and damaged organism. Regardless of which stage of the process we are in, we are moving in the direction of healing.

Direction is more important than speed.

Our soul is the subtlest yet the most potent part of our being that holds the power to heal. In this place, healing is a harmonious existence of our inner and outer world. Let's say that our soul is the same as our spirit. Spirituality is the path of connecting with our Spirit, and we experience healing as a result of this connection. So, Spirituality is the same as the path of healing.

We are Spiritual Beings in the human body because we come from the Universal Spirit or

Consciousness. Healing is a process of connecting with that Truth and becoming whole again while living our human life. Our struggles lessen, life becomes more enjoyable, and we begin to resonate with ourselves. Our past conditioning and beliefs naturally shed away, and changes become more internally driven rather than externally imposed as we begin to live this Truth more and more.

This changes our internal environment, energy, and vibration, and the outer life simply mimics that internal vibration. The obstacles we once perceived merely make way for our calling/purpose/mission that leads to happiness and joy. Whether eating, sleeping, or working, everything we do deeply aligns with our Truth.

In our daily lives, without creating a connection, we quickly get derailed and disconnected and mistakenly think that what we feel or witness is the truth of things. Falsely believing that we are broken, the ego blames the self (the ego self) without really understanding what the Self (The Soul Self) is. And we spend our entire lifetime fixing that blame and getting nowhere.

We are bound by the dense physicality of our being, mistakenly taking it as the only and whole of our being. Our physical body is a vessel, a container of the energy Source within us; we may say that our body is the tool for connecting with that Source.

Health and Healing

When we think of good health, we often relate it to our physical body only. As long as we are symptom-free, we are in good health. Many unhappy people are in good physical health; everything seemingly is okay, but nothing is. Doctors can't find any diagnosable condition, so they are sent home with an antidepressant or something like that. What's wrong is our disconnect from our Soul. Our physical symptoms and mental/emotional turmoil result from that disconnect, and left unattended for a long time shows up as a disease in the physical body. That's why looking at illness at the level of the symptoms seldom resolves it.

Healing is a much bigger and deeper process of aligning our physiology to our psychology. Psychology has a much bigger context in the Holistic realm than it does in conventional psychology. Here aligning means connecting with the deepest part of our being, and good health is the byproduct of that connection.

Disease is 100% energetic. It's our energy that gets sick before our body does. To heal is to reconnect with our Source – as this is the root cause level. Healing the energies of past experiences gives us a new level of awareness that catalyzes new beliefs, choices, and actions that are health-promoting. When we change that one thing in that more profound place, changes begin to cascade into every area of our life. Even the slightest shift will have a profound effect, just like a bit of stir at the bottom of the ocean can create tidal waves.

Healing is built-in, and healing is our human journey on this planet. During this significant shift, our wounds are resurfacing and beckoning for attention; we must look within and heal or risk spiralling downward endlessly.

We have spent enough time fixing, improving, and navigating the web of societal conditioning, which has fed into us the belief that we are inherently broken. We weren't told the truth because no one else knew it either, or at least they had forgotten it.

We get to be the Truth tellers for our next generation.

We chased this goal outside of ourselves and came back empty-handed. The truth is we are whole at the very core of our existence. The process now is to undo the doing and is more of self-discovery than of self-improvement.

The Wisdom of Triggers

Are you getting triggered lately?

Seriously? Do you even need to ask?

The natural response is to give it to them, tell them off, and boy, does it feel good, if only temporarily. Our world is not going to run out of triggers any time soon. So, it will serve us to get a deeper understanding and find our peace.

Here is the more profound understanding. Whatever is triggering us is what we haven't healed within ourselves. I know! It sucks!

Triggers are our response mechanism telling us that our nervous system is out of whack. We have myriad experiences in our human life, much of which we seldom resolve or digest. We ignore, move forward, and do life until triggered. Triggers are a reminder that we need to digest past experiences. All the unresolved experiences are hanging out in our subconscious garbage bin that needs emptying.

Not everyone is triggered by the same things, and not everyone is triggered with the same intensity. Our triggers are unique to us.

It is not about what is triggering you; rather, it's about what's triggering within you.

Triggers are little messengers asking us to pay attention. We may not like these little buggers, but they are necessary tools for us to heal. What within us needs healing is what we get triggered with.

Triggers are required to access our subconscious garbage bin.

As long as we are in human life, this garbage bin will never be empty, but it does not need to be stuffed to the rim either.

With our busy lives, we are engrossed in the "doing" and rarely take time to digest or reflect upon our life. So, the undigested experiences continue to accumulate in the subconscious. Left unattended for an extended period, they empty out on our body as disease in their final attempt to grab our attention. We don't have to wait that long; we can start sooner.

Everything that triggers us during these times is all that we have neglected in our past. We are merely reacting to the current situations and viewing them through the narrow lens of our undigested experiences. These experiences wait in the subconscious garbage bin to be digested and resolved. It's precisely these experiences that operate like a narrow lens through which we view our current reality and mistakenly think it's the current reality that's creating an upheaval in our lives when in fact, it's our past experiences that dictate our everyday behaviour and run the show.

The truth is our soul is and remains intact throughout our traumas or undigested experiences. (I am defining trauma as any experience we don't know what to do with) Healing is the profound realization of that truth. This realization must occur within the body, and it takes its own time. We are complex beings with thoughts, feelings, experiences, opinions, and we must travel through them as they are part of the body.

Healing spares all of our life force that we had vested in enduring the pain for our precious purposeful life.

Healing is an Organic Process

Healing is neither willed nor forced. What needs healing shows up naturally to our awareness. We can either ignore this awareness or pay attention to it and do the work required.

When I started introducing and offering Ayurvedic therapies in my practice, one client wanted to do them, thinking she might find something. Although it's lovely to experience, it seemed as though she was on a quest to uncover something for curiosity's sake. I asked whether anything was coming up for her that indicated something more. She said no. I suggested that she wait, "we don't' go digging for trouble; if life is working per your current satisfaction, then leave it alone."

When we deliberately go searching, we are in our heads, creating meaning out of things unnecessarily. This is called paralysis of analysis, which is sometimes common in conventional psychology. We could spend our entire life with that nonsense, but what would be thc point?

Healing is an organic process; we don't need to plan it. Healing is not a one problem - one solution deal. In my work with clients, I don't create a healing schedule; they show up with what needs their attention. I get a sense in my meditations which I realize later during the appointment. When we are open to energy, we begin to get a sense of what's to come and simply get out of the way. This is how life works; we follow what shows up, we don't will something to show up. Healing is allowed, and it's a skill we practice to get better at.

At times, I have noticed fear or resistance in new clients to start the work. They fear that they will not be able to handle the process and are scared of being overwhelmed. This has never happened. The truth is nothing shows up that we are not ready to handle. If it does show up, it's because we are prepared to handle it. This is the intelligence of our inner being; it always has our back.

Healing Happens in the Heart

We have been in the mental flow in our lives; here, ego/mind has been in charge, and we may have understood healing at an intellectual level. We are in the process of travelling to our heart; this is the process of ascension, a process of becoming a 5th Dimensional being, as I will explain later.

Healing must be experiential, as this is the only way to shift into a new state of being. This experience happens in the body via our heart. Our consciousness expands in our hearts. Healing happens in the heart, not in the mind.

We can't be in our mind and Expanded Consciousness at the same time.

When we talk about trauma, we are talking about its energies, as I will discuss in the next part of this book. This energy is in the body, so healing must be experienced where the trauma is stored, in the body. Our heart is the way to access the body.

Healing is a process of growth and wholeness. Wholeness resides deep in our hearts; the underlying field of energy and intelligence that directs all of life also directs the body's intelligence and all of its cells. In Ayurveda, this intelligence is Pure Consciousness. The heart is the container that not only witnesses all of our experiences but is also the gateway to access this Pure Consciousness. The amazing nature of Consciousness, in itself, is purifying and rejuvenating. It is in Its nature to bring wholeness.

The heart is the most prominent part of our body. Ego argues but our heart is a place of pure knowing. The nature of the heart is to unite all abandoned parts of ourselves to wholeness.

No one can hurt our heart so there is no need to guard our heart but from our own mind.

The stuff in the heart is the stuff of our mind's making. A broken heart is an expanded heart and open heart, and it shuts down from input from the mind. Fear comes from the mind; the heart only knows love. The work of healing is about love lived and made visible, so it begins to permeate within us and radiate through us. This is possible. This is available.

Shame, blame, and guilt are all constructs of the mind placed in the heart as a byproduct of our trauma, as the mind does not know what to do with it. The heart simply witnesses this like an innocent child witnessing the arguing parent. The patterns are of the psyche and mind. The heart can only expand. The heart responds to pain and joy in the same way as receiving the light can feel the same as receiving the negativity; there is an impulse. The heart responds by opening; pain breaks our heart open, but we shut it with the mind from fear of more pain.

The times we are in provide all the material to work through and come to the wholeness of Love. This is THE lifetime to heal all the prior lifetimes and truly start a new life free from the past traumas and conditioning. We can release all that; when we heal, we heal the wounds of generations, end the family karma and spare our children the family fate that we may have inherited.

This is the time to travel to the heart and get to know the healing power of the heart.

The Extraordinary Human

Our power to choose is a gift; it's our superpower. But sadly, most of us are asleep to this power and don't understand how to use it. We can choose love; we can choose to trust the unknown; we can choose to see the opportunity for growth instead of wallowing in the worry. We have a choice. Understanding the enormity of it will make us conscious of our choices.

Our second superpower is our ability to imagine, which we underutilize. Nothing unreal can ever be imagined. Imagining it brings it into existence. What future can you imagine for yourself?

These powers are like treasures that will produce miraculous results for humanity when tapped into. These abilities hold the power to make us into the possible human, as Dr. Jean Houston calls it. Our superpowers are built-in Divine Gifts that we have forgotten living in a 3D world (explained later) where the ego's limitations zapped our energy and kept these superpowers hidden from our conscious mind. These times offer a stark contrast to make us tap into these powers to create peace, ease, and joy. This is a conscious and deliberate work if we don't want to fall prey to the default way of fear and anxiety.

To claim these superpowers is also to take radical responsibility for everything we experience in our life. Once we take responsibility, the opportunities for healing will surface; this is where we can make another choice to stay present, to listen, and to awaken.

We don’t choose superficially. Knowing we have a choice is one thing, but doing the inner work to back up that choice is the whole deal. No amount of convincing the mind that “I am Okay” when the internal environment is screaming, “No, I am not,” will be enough and only creates more internal conflict and turmoil. This turmoil is a little messenger for transformation if we pay attention and choose it. Remember, our conflict is NEVER with others, but it shows up as such simply mirroring the internal strife. The task then is to connect deeply with what is heartfelt, having the courage to feel what we feel. This spares our energy to heal rather than to control. This is not about making believe or about parroting affirmations. (They may provide temporary relief, but don't create lasting results). When we go to the root of suffering and work at that level, we eradicate suffering for good. Healing is about creating an inner state that does not fluctuate with life fluctuations. Without that type of inner work, we forever remain at the mercy of our circumstances, and we don't need to. This is our ultimate human journey.

Healing is an Inward Journey

We need transformation, not more information or knowledge. Information is one-dimensional; transformation takes place internally where the experience happens. Our inner world is non-linear. That's why it is easier to achieve success and not easy to be happy. We can't use the outer model to solve inner conflicts. We must enter the inner world of healing and wholeness.

An internally driven life can be a tough road at times. Where is the "bliss" that we thought we were promised on this journey? We never really know until we "know". I know it sounds like a bunch of codified words, and they are, indeed, as the definition or the meaning can only be given by the one who experiences it. This path requires a different kind of resilience. How is this useful when fear and anxiety is an everyday experience for many of us? What do we do with all the darkness and negativity that shows up vehemently again and again?

If we are "love and light," then why do we continuously experience fear and darkness?

Do we ignore it? Pretend it away? Focus on all the positives we have in our lives? Accept it? Let go of it? Instead of wanting what we want, how about if we ask what's needed of us in the dark times?

Darkness is a part of the light. In trying to chase the darkness away, we forget that the light will lose its meaning without it. We have separated the light from darkness for the last 7 billion years. This is the time for fear to dance together with love, for light and darkness to coexist. Love is the highest force and holds the fear within it, for fear and darkness can’t exist by themselves; they exist when there is a lack of love and light. One-sided love needs to open to its counterpart for it to be whole. We have to be open to pain to know love. In our flow of love, the Divine enters.

We are the solution; when we heal, we heal the whole of humanity.

We don’t need to make sense of the nonsenses in the world; we need to accept it within ourselves. What's asked of us is to transmute the fear and darkness and turn it into love and light. This happens when we travel inward.

We may not see what's inside. We work with what we can't see. We know what's in front of us; we can't see the blueprint of the energies that are seeking to be freed within us. That energy remains, even though our memory and vision have been shut down. Our experiences are based on those energies.

Our planet is like the jewel in the fire getting transformed. The potential of this lifetime is incredible. We assist significantly as we transform ourselves; when our presence becomes an expansive beam of light that our world needs.

Mind was used as a tool for darkness. Heart, in its original design, is meant to lead the way. We can stand in the middle of this fire, with our arms and hearts open and flow love to it, pulling in all the opposites and bringing it to wholeness. This is a new way. The path is inward.

Outer World Reflects Our Inner Experiences

There is no darkness "out there" without it being "in here"; we must first realize that. Before spending so much of our energy chasing the darkness that we think is outside, we must realize it is nothing more than what's inside. The world outside mirrors the world inside. The "bad people and things" represent our demons and fears. Our inner world creates a filter through which we see the outer world, and most of the time, it can create a veil in front of our eyes as we fail to "see."

We have been leaving our energetic imprints in this world. Living in the fear and ego-based realm, chasing everything outside of us, enduring pain and suffering; the dark energies of these experiences is what is in our planet. The accumulation of these energies is what's showing up in a big way to be cleared. This understanding is a way out of our suffering as we can change/heal what's "in here," and thank God; we don't have to fix or change anything "out there". The inner work is about healing our past traumas and wounds, expanding the love, so we can radiate it "out there".

Our life experiences become the source of our happiness if we heal from them.

The task on hand is to transmute our darkness and fear into light and love. Loving and completely accepting our darkness can transmute our fears rather quickly. This may happen in layers; as you know, internal work is an unending step process; it happens in layers. The good news is that it happens at the perfect time when we are in dire need of it and when we can handle it.

Let's not buy into "the world is so bad right now" that quickly, even though I know it is. Remember, we have a choice. There are equally good things happening in the world. The world is undergoing a much-needed shift, and it is working. How do we know it’s working? Crazy becomes crazier. No need to make sense of the nonsense or to rationalize the irrational. Go within because that’s where our power is. And hold trust for that Supreme Intelligence to bring our world back into balance, and it will. We simply keep our focus on our healing.

It's our personal darkness that shows up in the collective. Right now, we are in the messy middle. Let's not mistake the process for the end result. Even if you think you have no fear, start going inward, and fear will show up as it is as much a part of you as love. Transmuting our fear at every step will go far in changing the world "out there."

There is no "them," it's all "us." That's the reality; separation is in our perception only. It's our inner reality that is showing up on the external. The external is simply the mirror reflecting what we don't want to see. So, let's show IT something different. Let's show IT what we want to be reflected.

Healing is Clear Seeing

So much of how we live and what we think and believe results from our experiences that we haven't yet metabolized. These experiences are traumas with a little t. We also experience major Trauma like death, divorce, accident, or other natural disasters. Healing is digesting or positively dealing with these experiences. Without healing, our entire way of living is in response to those undigested experiences.

When we withdraw from others, become hyper-vigilant, become passive-aggressive, and get triggered due to unhealed trauma, we respond to life from our traumatised self. *A client was worried about her elderly mother, who stopped taking care of herself, wasn't taking her medications, and was surviving on just tea and bread. She thought that would end her life sooner than later. What's the point of my living? She lost all interest in life. She had recently lost her husband of 60 years, who kept her occupied by taking care of him. Her purpose was to take care of him. The traumas she experienced in her life were so alive that she shut down so she could not feel the pain of her life, but she also shut down to all the possibilities that her life still held for her. She forgot what she enjoyed; she forgot her dreams and desires.*

Healing our past removes all the layers we accumulate to stay safe. This is a built-in response, but there comes a time when we no longer need it. Even when we have landed safely in our life, our psyche is on autopilot, always protecting us even when it does not need to. We remain blinded to our true nature, passions, and purpose in life. This is when we have to retrain ourselves in trusting life once again consciously. This is healing.

Healing is clear seeing into our gifts and our purpose. Purpose is to the soul like food is to the body; it is our soul pulse, our lifeline that keeps our inner fire burning and gives meaning to our life.

We all have gifts to share in this world, and healing is a must if we want to have access to this "knowing"; healing is not a luxury but necessary to uncover our true North.

How Long Does Healing Take?

One of the most miraculous things about being human is that we can be suffering for our entire life, but when we decide to heal, it happens rather quickly. If you have been suffering for decades, you don't need to take decades to heal. As I mentioned earlier, healing is a process of becoming whole, becoming our true selves, but whatever stage of healing you are in, you feel more whole than before. Life becomes better than you had realized or known before at every stage.

I have worked with people in their 60's and 70's who had been carrying the burden of unresolved experiences (trauma and Trauma) their whole life, but once they woke up to the knowledge that their life was not working and decided to heal, they did rather quickly. I have witnessed this over and over again. No matter how severe the trauma and for how long you have been holding it, you can heal.

A single ray of light can disperse the darkness of the entire space. In much the same way, the power of healing is a much bigger force than any trauma.

We are whole at the core of our being; our inner being is always waiting to reveal that to us.

So, in this healing process, we are not looking to get to the finish line because there isn't one. Rather it's a delightful, messy, painful, engaging, and awakening journey that takes us closer and closer to who we were uniquely designed to be and called to do. This is quite an adventure far more interesting than what's happening in the outer world; this journey gives you your life back and your energy back to live fully.

In this process, you lose interest in rehashing the past, holding on to grudges, engaging in conflict; but hold more interest in finding peace, sharing love, creating, awakening to the beauty of this life and this planet.

The secret of healing is the same as the secret of all success; what you think is what you get. If you expect that you will never heal from past trauma, then you won't. If you believe, as I do, that we can heal from anything and everything, then that would show up as true for you. "Think you can or think you can't, and either way, you'll be correct."

Healing doesn't ask whether you have been in pain for 25 minutes or 25 years. It is always available in the NOW moment. Consider two rocks that have been submerged underwater in a streambed; one has been submerged for 10,000 years and the other for ten days. If you place both rocks in the sun, they will take the same amount of time to dry off.

Our culture has instilled within us many beliefs about who and what can be healed and how long it takes. This is the philosophy of our conventional medical world; you just have to live with it, you are getting old, this is common in people your age, take these pills, blah blah blah. Many of these beliefs are based on limiting thoughts to which other people have subscribed. If you do not think the same thoughts, you are not subject to the same results. With statistics of what happens to people who exhibit the same symptoms as you, they simply note how other people have dealt with this issue. What you do with it may be entirely different, and you are not bound to have the same result. The only thing that determines where you land is the train of thought you take to get there. Step onto a different train, and you will arrive at a different station.

Healing only cares about our willingness; it does not discriminate against anything. We are good enough to experience the gift of this human life, and we are all good enough to heal.

Examine your beliefs about how long you think healing should take. How long have you been putting up with pain or a situation that is not working? How long have you not had use of a part of your life that you would rather enjoy? What do you think needs to happen before you can feel good? How long are you willing to suffer in that toxic relationship? Are you worthy enough to heal?

The truth is nothing outside of us needs to change for us to be who we are designed to be, to heal, to become whole, to follow our heart, and to fulfil our purpose.

Our opportunities to heal never end, and there is never any judgement on how long it takes.

Be a Spiritual Warrior

To be spiritual is to ask bigger questions and to look at the bigger picture. In that bigger context, you will see that whatever is happening to you is happening for you. The craziness in the external world, which is trying desperately to figure out how to control humanity, is a play of the ego on its last hurrah, forgetting that it's creating an invisible opposition force and fueling it. Just what we need! To wake up and take a stand. We live in a polarized world; the energies of control can either give rise to the energy of fear or of freedom. As Spiritual Warriors, we are not rebelling against anyone outside of us; we are fighting our inner darkness to become sovereign. We become steadfast in ourselves, power, and values and live from that place. We see everyone else sovereign, and accept them completely because we know every being is God incarnated; every experience is God experiencing the human-ness. We see God in all.

The objective of this path is not to have an easy life but to have an awakened and meaningful life.

The point is not to win or lose, be right or wrong, but rather to heal and bring unity to all the abandoned parts of ourselves. Here we see that there is no "them." There is only "us." Our heart longs for unity, and this is how we live in Unity Consciousness.

The point is to stand in our Sovereignty, question everything, and fear nothing.

As spiritual warriors, we are not naive; we protect and honour our energy. We know to take care of ourselves physically, mentally, emotionally, and spiritually so we can continue to be the conduit, the beacon of Love. We know our world needs us.

Three months into the pandemic, zoom became my entire office; it finally sunk in that I wouldn't be returning to the office any time soon. I was witnessing life shifting in ways I wasn't prepared for. Many clients only wanted in-person appointments, so they took a break until I returned to the office. Like all of us, I didn't know where to land or what to do. This is when I surrendered myself to the big question; why am I living through these times? What's being asked of me? Next thing

I knew, I was spending countless hours on social media, teaching about spirituality, leading meditations, leading many healthy living projects with the Michigan Indian Community Services (MICS), as well as teaching many free webinars on mental and emotional health. All of a sudden, everyone needed what I was offering. Everyone became interested in immunity and Ayurveda. I lugged all the herbs from my office, ordered more, and there I was in my kitchen making immunity packs for people. I felt like an alchemist with herbs everywhere, mixing bowls, computer open, and client forms to fill the order. I was witnessing myself and smiling. Suddenly, conventional medicine had no answer. Just like that, everyone wanted these immunity packs. I felt like a warrior. I had to do all I knew to do to help others. This was what I was called to do. Just like I am being called to write this book. I have my phone turned off, and there is nothing on my mind other than to finish this book. When we ask the bigger questions, the answers come through us, and we can't stop them. That's when you know the Source is working through you. This is the path of a Spiritual Warrior".

Can we make a difference to one person? Can we offer acceptance and compassion to one person? Can we be the mirror of someone's goodness? What do we have that the world needs?

Here, our stories are going to heal more than our degrees.

Our big-heartedness is needed more than our small minds. What we can do for others will hold more weight than what we have studied or achieved. It's our ego that thinks I have to accomplish something massive in order to be noticed. At the heart level, we are not concerned with being noticed; rather, we notice and truly see others. At this level, kindness and love are not measured. No heart action is big or small; it carries the same high energy that our world needs.

As I sit in my zoom office in Toronto, with all the degrees and credentials stored away somewhere, I show up fully for my clients, and they notice, and that's what makes a difference in their lives. They no longer see any certificates hanging on the wall behind, and they don't care.

Ask yourself why you are living through these times? It’s no coincidence. We are meant to show others the way. God is working through you and me to light the path for humanity.

In asking the bigger question, we develop our higher faculties like intuition. Intuition is our inborn ability to tap into the energetic world and see the unseen. Our ego blocked these built-in abilities. We are energetic beings; our power lies in our subtleties. To hang out with the question and sit in the possibility of what might be is the way to strengthen our connection to our Higher Self and our intuition. What more is here that I may not be seeing? Asking will open the mind and the intuition to see beyond and into what's happening. The biggest question is: "Who Am I?" and can take us into our full potential as beings and set up the platform for healing.

Uncovering Mysteries of Healing

Healing is mysterious because whatever unfolds we never saw coming. We connect the dots in ways that we never realized. The awareness sneaks upon us, and we are awestruck and dumbfounded at the same time. No matter how much we heal, there is always more. We only know what we know, and we don't know what we don't know.

Healing is a continuous mysterious dance between the known and the unknown.

When we ask the questions to provoke our inner knowing, answers show up. *One of the questions I always ask my clients is, "why do you think you have the health issues you are having?" This makes them think beyond the symptoms, and the connection of the symptoms to their life story begins to emerge; not only that, they begin to see how the same story is playing in other areas of their life - in their work, in their relationships, and their health. Simply the willingness to look beyond the physical symptoms raises their awareness level, and they begin to see a bigger picture than they had before. That in itself is empowering and begins the healing process at the level of their awareness.*

More times than not, the disease or the symptoms tell a story of our life, especially the unresolved one.

The only way to resolve or heal the story is to go into its experience, details are relevant to a point, but it is the experience that continuously repeats in other areas of our life and in our illness. We feel the need to share our story repeatedly, making it more dramatic each time. It's always a story of what someone did, how awful they were, and how they become more awful each time we share the story. In this way of living, we recreate our experiences and retraumatize ourselves. We must shift our focus to our own experiences because there is information there that can help us heal. We take ownership of our experiences, dig deeper and begin the healing process.

When we realize that we have the power to change our story, we begin to heal.

Healing is simple and complex at the same time. It isn’t, however, easy. I think that in the next ten years, it will become easier, as we will hold more consciousness where we can naturally access the deeper layers.

This work isn't easy, it requires a certain kind of stamina, but it is easier than living with an illness. You may experience resistance in different ways; rationalization, make-believe, or pretending that all is okay when it isn't. Fear shows up in all sorts of distorted ways. This is where you may need expert guidance to help you through it.

Our circumstances do not define us. Every day we heal addictions, past trauma, physical illnesses, and these inspirational stories are everywhere for us to see and get inspired and believe in our own healing. Time after time, I share these teachings in my practice with miraculous results. I live these teachings, and they continue to transform my life in ways I could never have imagined. You too, can heal and overcome all the blocks in the process. I hold that belief for you. Can you hold that belief for yourself?

Illness happens by default, healing is chosen.

Healing is Always for the Collective

My work is very personal to me. This type of work seldom comes from a book, rather it comes from our own direct personal experiences. I write this book from my experiences to teach and to share with you.

I have experienced many tragedies, traumas, and all the human emotions that we as humans experience in this life. That's how I am able to connect deeply with the pain of others because I have been there. I am the "lab" of what I teach; it goes through me; it works me without any mercy. I jokingly tell my clients that they better pay attention because I have been to hell and back to crystallize the teachings for them. After each dark night of the ego, I have shed light on another layer of my making, my soul, and naively thinking that I am now done. We are never done. Healing is a journey to get to know ourselves. How can we ever be done? The mystery of who we are unfolds with time, keeping us awestruck and fascinated for the next layer of our unfolding.

I “see” my clients through their pain just like I “see” myself through mine. I am the example for you, for you to know that you too can heal from anything and overcome any obstacles that come in the way. I share my story in my work to offer connection, hope, and inspiration. To each passing experience, I question what is being asked of me. This is when everything becomes available to me. Frankly, I don’t know how to live any other way.

I hope many get to read this book. Am I just full of myself with a hidden agenda of getting famous? No! But you are free to be the judge of it. My agenda is to inspire you to heal. Why? So, you also can inspire thousands of others. Do you see how when we heal, we heal others with our stories, our presence, and creating a tidal wave of healing across our globe? This already is happening in our world. This is also spreading like a virus. Let’s all catch THIS virus.

Healing is highly contagious. When we heal, we heal those around us, we heal our families, our communities, our cities, our countries, and our world. This is how we become the conduit of love. This is your calling: this is why you are living through these times. This is how we serve humanity; this is how we become messengers of GOD. This is the ultimate Yoga, to serve the greatest and to love the deepest.

Our wounds aren't for nothing. We didn't suffer for nothing. There were lessons in them. Let's not normalize pain and suffering, it isn't why we are here. We are here to heal, to awaken to that yearning, that fire within each one of us. Nothing creates a bigger burden for our souls than our unfulfilled dreams and desires. Can you imagine the healing impact you can have on the world with your story?

Have I inspired you to do the deep work to find that hidden gem within you? If yes, I rest my case and needn't add anything more here to convince you that a more significant purpose awaits you in your healing.

The Cry for Connection

These are peculiar times for sure. On one hand, I crave the in-person social connection. On the other hand, it's hard to find a match for my vibe. We have all become ultrasensitive; in some small or big way, we got wounded during this time. We are all protecting our energetic territories but not without feeling isolated. The truth is we are not quite sure where to land yet.

Zoom connections feel safe at the moment for most of us. But this can't be the way. One of the aspects my clients miss most is hugs and a shared cup of tea; hard to do that on Zoom. Getting together with others, freely going to visit friends, freely meeting for coffee or to watch a show is all that we took for granted and now feels like a dream. How wonderful it would be to do all that.

In the meantime, during this time of isolation, we are asked to connect with ourselves. Yes, this is an excellent time for deep inner work. We are asked to travel inward first to fulfil that need for connection. The truth is we have all experienced loneliness even in the middle of big gatherings because the yearning for deep connection is first fulfilled within ourselves. Disconnected from ourselves, we have spent years chasing social gatherings to no avail.

Imagine the level of presence we bring into a group when we are deeply connected, in our center, and in our sovereignty. That's when we are totally received. When the connection is from the inside out, it fills your heart and the heart of those around you like nothing else. Spending this time to do the inner work, feeling deeply connected to ourselves will serve us well. Imagine the richness and fullness we will experience when we do get to freely socialize.

So much healing will be experienced when we do come together in our shared stories and shared humanity. The truth is a connection to oneself and connection with others is simply healing. Connection and support lay a solid foundation for our deep healing. All addictions come from disconnection; as we subconsciously seek to fill a gap and quiet down that inner voice, the inner revolution, the inner unrest but only temporarily.

We can see this happening in our world today as a result of the isolation and disconnect.

We have been conditioned to not ask for help, to pretend we have all we need, to be strong even when we are falling apart inside. We need to let go of shame, guilt in asking for love, for connection. The animals have no judgement; the cat rolls on her back so you can keep scratching her belly, the dog keeps sniffing you or chasing you until you pay attention. *Growing up, I used to comb the hair of my calf as he would lay his head in my lap and would push me down with his head as I tried to get up. He needed more loving; little did he know (or he did know) that I was feeling equally loved if not more.*

There is a need for a deep connection with our heart and its needs; a need to let go of the ego and become real and transparent. This need is fulfilled when we do the inner healing work.

We Don't Heal in Isolation

The fact that mental health issues have become an epidemic during this time is not a coincidence. The isolation that we have all experienced and continue to experience is adding to our mental health challenges.

Needless to say, physical social interactions are tricky during this time. However, I also know that there is a lot of online socialization that is happening during this time. It will never be a replacement but can be hugely beneficial for our mental and social health.

We don't and can't heal in isolation; we need guidance, teachers, mentors, friends, and here is why. There is witness value in being in the presence of another. We feel heard, received, and validated; we are witnessed. This, in itself, is healing.

We don't heal sitting in a room alone. As much as the healing work is internal and personal, we need a witness, a guide to walk us through the path.

“Rarely, if ever, are any of us healed in isolation. Healing is an act of communion.” Bell Hooks

A Shift in Consciousness

Before I explain the shift, let's first understand Consciousness.

Consciousness is Universal Energy and Life Force in its purest or unmanifest form devoid of duality; hence, the term Pure Consciousness. This Consciousness is full of information and intelligence.

Our journey into the physical body begins with Consciousness, just like a tree begins with the seed; it is the Source of our Being. However, it transcends human life; in other words, it does not end when our human life ends. It has no beginning and no end and is beyond the concept of time and space. Our human body is designed to be the vessel for this Energy; it exists in us and outside of us.

As infants and young children below the age of 5, we are deeply in connection with this Energy which shows up in our experience as love, laughter, joy, and innocence. As we get older and step into our human experiences, we get disconnected from this Energy. We experience pain, suffering, and disease of both body and mind. This is our experience of being in the 3rd Dimension of Consciousness (3D); much of our humanity has been operating from this state of Consciousness.

3D is a state of Consciousness; here, we experience fear, confusion, conflict, emotional upheaval, lack of sense of self, overwhelm, separation, and disconnection; we have no awareness of what's happening inside or outside of us. You may say we are sleep-walking. In this state of Consciousness, we believe we are just bodies and are always at the effect of our circumstances. Disconnected from our inner resources and guidance, we search for solutions outside of ourselves.

5D is a higher state of Consciousness. Here we understand that we are more than the physical body; we feel connected to Pure Consciousness. We trust our inner guidance and intuition. We feel a connection to the whole Creation and naturally tune in to the other energetic realms; we understand we are multidimensional. All is one in this state of existence, and we experience this Oneness within ourselves. Living in 5D Consciousness, we experience peace, love, and harmony.

Higher or lower states of Consciousness are relative to the state we are in at any given time in our life. It's worth mentioning that this is not about creating a hierarchy amongst us; it's rather about understanding the nature of this Energy.

The Shift is the process of becoming a 5th Dimensional Being. This is where we are headed as a collective. In simpler words, we are moving from fear to love, from darkness to light, from separation to unity, and this is how we are birthing the New World.

The technique that you will learn in the last part of the book is the technique to shift into 5D. This is the technique to heal the pain of the past.

The 5D is not anything new. The ancients knew it, and that's how we lived millions of years ago. The oldest and time-tested system of health and longevity, the science of Pure Consciousness -

Ayurveda understood that we are multidimensional beings.

Human design is a design of co-creation and co-existence with the whole of Creation. Suspended between Mother Earth and Father Sky, we are the conduits of information and guidance from the Higher Realms so we can live following the guidance we receive. Living this way, we feel deeply connected and integrated; we experience wholeness, balance, and harmony.

Ours is a superior design, for we are given a mind. Over time, when we realized the power of our mind, we separated it from the rest of our being. There was no need to worry because with the mind we created, accomplished, and did unimaginable things. In this race, we forgot our heart, we forgot our connection with Creation, we moved further and further away from our True Nature. Greed and ego set in and we forgot who we were designed to be. We tried to outsmart and control Nature because we could. We created and destroyed at our own will and ignored the looming consequences and mistakenly thought we were in charge of the whole of Creation. Disconnected from ourselves, we ignored our failing health and lived in a state of imbalance.

Nature is continually working to maintain balance. The pandemic is nature's way to get us to pay attention, slow down and bring balance. We suffered the consequences of living an unbalanced life through the disease of the body and mind; the pain, fear, the disconnect that we ignored surfaced and we had to take notice.

Our world is undergoing that Shift. It's up to each one of us to create that shift within ourselves making this a very significant time in our lives. Instead of being passive passengers, each one of us can choose to be in the driver seat, directing humanity Home.

Healing the past wounds will lighten up the load on our soul and will naturally shift us into the experiences of love, peace, and harmony. The shift from 3D to 5D is also called Ascension, the shortest and longest distance from our head to our heart. The shift is the remembrance of who we are and coming home to ourselves. This is the process of healing.

We have all suffered in the hands of our own limited mind/ego; in the 5D we no longer need to suffer. Our inner mental structures are breaking apart to make way for the new way of thinking, living, and being. We are freeing ourselves from the shackles of the past conditioning. We are born free; we can live free. This is the promise of 5D.

Part II

About Energy

Meena Puri

What is Energy?

We are both physical and non-physical beings. We tend to think of our body as just physical; the non-physical part of our being is a sub-stratum of the physical body. For the purpose of this book, our non-physical body is our mental body (our thoughts), our emotional body (our feelings), and our energy body (chakra system). Our thoughts and feelings are energetic impulses; we can't show our thoughts or feelings to someone, but we can feel them, and so can others.

Our energy is not confined in our physical body; it can be experienced by others even when they are not in our physical proximity. Energy can travel almost at the speed of light and therefore is not bound by time. We may not be aware of other people's energy, but we are susceptible to it. Notice how you feel after spending some time with a friend who is continuously complaining and angry. Notice how you feel when you are in the company of a positive and a happy friend.

One person with a high state of consciousness can shift the energy of the whole room filled with negativity. When we heal, we shift to a higher state of consciousness and, therefore, can help uplift others to a higher state of consciousness.

I am not suggesting that you surround yourself with negativity and darkness without protecting your own energy so you can influence others positively rather than get drawn into the lower state of consciousness, which can and does happen. You can draw a circle around you and set the intention that you are energetically safe. Energy follows our intention and attention, and this is how we can shift and direct our energy.

Our every thought, feeling, and action creates an energetic impulse, and our feelings and thoughts result from the energetic impulses that we carry within us. Every single thing, living or inanimate, is made up of energy. It's all vibrating, and frequency is the rate of its vibration. Lower negative emotions and thoughts are of lower vibration, and higher positive emotions are of higher vibration.

Energy is not linear; there is no beginning or end. It is cyclical; what we put out into the world is what we receive back. Karma is the energy of action and reaction; what we sow, we shall reap;

what goes around comes around. Karma is neither a punishment nor a reward; it's what we have created with our actions, thoughts, and feelings.

We are not separate from these energies because we are a part of them, and they are a part of us, and they are waiting for us to give them their freedom.

Life reflects who we are.

Everything we are experiencing in our life mirrors a part of us that is ready to know Love. We may be a victim in a situation; however, the situation mirrors some part of us that is crying to know Love, and it requires us to acknowledge and fully accept these energies for them to heal. If we genuinely want to experience freedom in our life, we have to choose to open our hearts to Love and to all that life presents to us. This is how we free the energies.

Instead of thinking of ourselves in terms of how we feel, such as fearful or angry, we can think about the energy of fear and anger. This keeps us from judging ourselves and others and gives us a bigger perspective.

The source of our beingness is Pure Consciousness. Our being (physical and non-physical) is the translation of that Pure Consciousness. When we talk about getting to the root of disease, we are talking about the energetics of the disease. Our energy gets sick before our body does.

Different organs store different emotions and, when unresolved, can lead to disease of that organ. Unresolved anger is associated with the liver, unresolved grief for the lungs and perceived lack of love leads to heart issues.

Merely treating the symptoms may prolong our life due to modern medicine's tremendous advancements; however, healing comes from diving to the root cause and making changes there. All disease is a disconnection from the Source, leading us to feel isolated and separated from love. This is our perception only, as we are the source of that Love that we seek. Healing is a connection with our Source. Therefore, being symptom-free and healing are two very different concepts.

What our world needs is healing.

What is God?

I dare not try to explain what GOD is. I can, however, share how I think of GOD. The truth is we can get lost in philosophy and arguments, but that's not the purpose of this book. I learned this definition of GOD - Generating, Organizing, and Destroying force that is always working to keep the world in balance. For the purpose of this book, GOD is Energy or Pure Consciousness.

In this context, GOD is the Source of Creation ITSELF. God is Consciousness, not independent of you and me. IT is the totality of everything. When I call myself God, I am not talking about my personal self; I am talking about the expression of GOD Self that rests inside me. IT'S a verb, not a noun.

When we think GOD is a person, a noun, or a thing, we separate ourselves from IT and become a limited being. We think GOD is out there, up in the sky. We look up as GOD is the most elevated energy not because there is a person sitting in the clouds. That's what separates the believers (Religious) from the knowers (Spiritual).

Feel free to think of GOD in ways that uplift you and help you to connect with this Energy. There is no right or wrong way; we are all allowed to have our own understanding of IT.

Energy Goes Round and Round

We may forget about energy, but energy does not forget us. It comes back again and again until we free it. Like I mentioned before, energy is non-linear, it continues on.

I lived in a small town in India, and we had no phone. There was one phone in the entire neighbourhood on which we received calls. Our family in Canada would call us on that phone once in a while. The neighbour would come upon the rooftop to tell us when there was a phone call, and I remember running across the rooftop, jumping on the ledge, then jumping into my neighbour's veranda and running into their living room to get the phone. Being the youngest, I was given this task as I could run fast.

The communication was mostly done via letters, and big news was shared by telegrams.

My brother Yash, his wife, and their son lived in Toronto, Canada, expecting their second child. We were all eagerly waiting for the news, and the news came. We got a telegram that read, "My sister-in-law left with a son." We understood that to mean that my sister-in-law died along with her newborn son. The full-fledged mourning started at my home with neighbours and relatives coming. Even professional mourners somehow showed up at the news (In India, upon someone's death, mourners are called to make sure that the family members cry and grieve and don't get stuck in the grief). I remember worrying about my young nephew as to who would raise him. Our family was devastated.

To call someone right away was neither convenient nor common. After many tries from the neighbour's house, we finally got connected. The telegram was wrong. It was meant to read, "My sister-in-law blessed with a son." The mourning changed into a celebration, and all was well.

A few years later my youngest brother (older to me), passed away in an accident not long after he graduated from medical school. A year after his death, my older brother Yash insisted that we all come to Canada, as we were still so grief-stricken. Before my younger brother's death, my father never considered coming to Canada. My brother's death left us very vulnerable, weak and broken, so my dad agreed, and we all came to Canada. We landed early in the morning, and the very day in the evening, my brother Yash, who invited us, died. He was lowering his younger son's bike (the same son who we thought had died along with his mother) from the balcony, and fell with the bike on the walkway to the front door, hit his head on the slabs that he had just placed there a few days ago to welcome us into his home.

My insight tells me that by falsely mourning for my sister-in-law and her newborn son, we set powerful energies in motion that circled our family. The energy of mourning for my sister-in-law somehow landed first on my brother in India and then followed us to Canada. These are seemingly two separate episodes, but I feel they are not. Is it possible that the false mourning created the real mourning? Energy is energy, it does not know what is real and what is not.

When our physical life ends, our energetic life carries on to the next lifetime. All the energies that are not resolved or healed will pass on to the next lifetime. *I share this with my clients who contemplate suicide, that whatever problems they are trying to get away from will follow them in the next lifetime. This makes them change their mind.*

We Only See Half of It

We can't see energy, but we can feel it.

Our every thought/feeling, conscious or subconscious, and every action creates energy. This we know. What we don't know or forget to consider is that energy within us creates the same energy outside of us.

For example, if your first thought in the morning is that it's another shitty day, you set forth the same energy outside that reinforces your thought. As you get out of bed with that thought, you may trip over something, the toilet may get plugged up, and there is no more toothpaste. In other words, the external reinforces your inner energy. How can we use this to our advantage? We can equally get up with a positive thought like it will be a fantastic day. Give it a try and see what happens.

But we need to understand more than that. It's not about what we say but how we truly feel inside. If we haven't done much looking within, we remain unaware of our own deeply buried feelings. If we agree that the external merely mirrors the internal, then our external experiences are a significant clue to what's happening inside of us. The truth is even with all the inner work; we can be blind-sided because our ego comes in the way of clear seeing. Because we live in a polarized world, the more conscious we become, the larger of a shadow (ego) we can have. That's why, it's always good to fall flat on our face once in a while, so we don't get ahead of ourselves. If we just parrot some affirmations without believing in them, we can continue to have a crappy day. It's the deep inner experience that gets mirrored, not what we say. There are no shortcuts to healing the inner terrains of our being.

The external responds to who we are, not what we say or what we want.

Our world is currently providing a great example. We can see the energies of fear, control, manipulation, victimhood, isolation, abandonment, etc. We have collectively created this external experience because we have experienced it internally for a long time. Energy always has a counterpart; there is no energy of fear without the energy of control and vice versa. We don't know which energy is created first, as it is all intertwined without a beginning or end. The energies we are experiencing in the world are old energies that all of us have experienced sometime along our soul's journey. We have an opportunity before us to heal these energies once and for all.

We are bound to others and our environment by an invisible field of energy. We affect others and are affected by others. With our presence alone, we leave an energetic imprint wherever we go. The question is, what imprint do we want to leave behind?

It's not about people; it's about the energy.

All of our experiences are energetic first, and there is always a counterpart to them. For example, the energy of victimhood exists only in the energy of the perpetrator. Where there are no perpetrators, there are no victims and vice versa. In that context, all truths are half-truths. We only see what is visible to our eyes; to see "into" a situation comes from our intuition.

Energy can neither be Created nor Destroyed

This is the first principle of energy. We bring these energies with us from our past lives. We don't create them in this life, nor can we destroy them. We can, however, transmute them. Consider the following example:

I became very fearful of dogs because one bit me when I was young. Then in my teens, anytime I saw a dog, I would start walking fast or sometimes running. Sensing my fear, the dog would bark harder and would chase me if he wasn't trained. When I understood that the dog was chasing me because I was running, I decided to stop running, still feeling fearful inside, I would walk in front of the dog as if I was not scared. The dog wasn't convinced. It read my fear and barked at me much the same way. Knowing that the dog would not chase me made me feel safer, so I started to walk slowly, looking at the dog. The dog softened and calmed down and stopped barking at me. As I write this, I realize I have come a long way when it comes to this fear of dogs. My old neighbourhood was filled with dogs, and they all knew me. I would talk to them, pet them and hang out with them. One of my neighbours would ask me to babysit their dog when they were away on vacation.

My first job as an accounting assistant was with this man who had a Doberman. He could not find anyone to work for him because of the dog. I got along with the dog just fine, and he hired me. We had to separate the dog in a room when the clients came, and it wasn't pretty opening the door to let him out when the client left. But I could handle him and calm him down. Who knows what's behind our fears? Maybe a part of us is waiting to be known? I had another job where my boss had a dog in the office. Brandy was the dog's name. The dog would put her head in my lap as I did my work and would not move her head away. I would dump all the files on her head, and she would remain there with her head buried in the files as I worked away. I literally would push her head off when I had to get up. I realized how much I love dogs. How my fear of dogs changed into love for them.

I didn't create fear, and I didn't destroy fear. I transmuted it into the energy of safety and trust.

We bring with us the energies of all prior lifetimes that we have not yet healed.

Where did it come from in the prior lifetime? I suppose, a lifetime before that and before that.

Where did it originate from?

From Source, from Pure Consciousness.

But Pure Consciousness is not fear. No, it isn't. Our human experiences alter this energy of Pure Consciousness into its lower expressions of human existence so we can experience being human and keep returning back to Pure Consciousness again and again. But why? Because GOD is having fun with us all. GOD is entitled since GOD created us.

This is the answer I made up. I don't know. How the heck will I know? No one knows where our soul journey begins and where it ends. And we have to be okay with it. Welcome to being human!

But what's not a mystery is that we come into this lifetime with the energies that are still needing to be healed. This explanation makes great sense to me and I hope it does to you too. I can live with this.

Our life on this planet is a continuum of all the lifetimes we have lived and our current experiences are representations of the energies we have created in prior lifetimes but haven't healed. Our current experiences are the ways that these energies get played out so we can see them, experience them and perhaps this time see into them and heal them. So, fear did not come from the pandemic, rather it activated the fear that has been there. Because not everyone is fearful, at least not to the same extent. Without understanding this, we believe we are doomed or are being punished instead of seeing the huge opportunity before us to heal all the past energies and karma. We don't need to know what happened in prior lifetimes; it is enough to know that our current experiences are not just limited to this lifetime.

A client continuously worried about getting cancer and directed all her efforts in preventing cancer. She could not understand this obsession with preventing cancer till I took her back to her mother's womb in a meditation. Then she remembered that her mother was diagnosed with cancer while she was pregnant with her.

Another client had so much focus on collecting food, making food, eating food because she said she was always feeling hungry and cold no matter the season and no matter how much food she consumed. This is exactly the feeling she had while being in her mother's womb – she brought this from a prior life to heal now.

We all experience fear to some extent and fear actually can save our lives but when we are paralyzed by fear, it will show up everywhere in our life. Regardless of how good life is, we may continue to fear losing our jobs, losing our relationships, being abandoned, or getting sick. At this time, when the energy of fear in our world is rampant, if you came into this life to heal the energy of fear, chances are you may experience it far more intensely than others as it has been the pattern in your life. Assess for yourself if that is true. The work is to transmute the energy of fear and this is what I will share with you in the last part of the book.

Energy Seeks Expression

Energy seeks freedom and needs its expression to be free. When we express anger, we feel better, at least for a little while. When we feel hurt, crying frees the energy of pain. When we feel happy, we laugh, share our happiness with others, sing or dance. We are expressing what we are feeling. But we can consciously choose a channel for our energy that not only frees it once and for all but expands us at the same time. That channel is LOVE. Love is the energy of the highest vibration, and all the lower vibration energies seek to be freed in Love.

Babies cry bloody murder when they are hungry. They use their entire body in the expression of it. There is no giggle like a baby's giggle. As adults, we forget to use our bodies to express our energy. That's why we can't just talk about healing, and it must be done somatically.

Our current times are a perfect setup for us to connect with the energy of Love. This is the broader view and has the solutions to our suffering. Our deep experiences within ourselves of feeling worthless, of suffering, of isolation, of loneliness, will continue to play out in our lives unless we free these energies. It is not a magic wand but rather a process; layer by layer we can free all the lower vibration energies into Love.

Love is the highest vibration that all energies seek to be expressed in creating deep healing. The saying, "Love heals all" is a true statement. Love is Oneness; there is no duality, this is where the opposites meet and realize they are more like each other than not. It's the meeting point not visible to us.

The healing is about experiencing this invisible union into our own hearts.

To heal these energies is to open our hearts to that part of us that is experiencing these energies and bringing them all into the ONE FLOW OF LOVE.

Did you know that Love is a much more powerful and stronger force than fear and that light is much more powerful than dark? A single ray of light lights up the whole room full of darkness. Choosing Love and Light is like betting on the winning horse. Why not choose Love and Light?

Disease is Unresolved Trauma and is 100% Energetic

Trauma is any experience that we have not yet metabolized. We experience many little traumas on a daily basis i.e., we have many experiences that we don't know what to do with. We watch the news, it creates fear. We quickly turn the news off, but trauma has already happened. We can't unsee or unhear what we already saw or heard. We try to ignore it; we push it away but the experience has already happened. It's a bit too late. Where is the experience of fear? It's stored in our body somewhere. We may forget about it, distract ourselves and move on. But the fear in the body remains and we are not aware of it. Now we are scared of watching the news, even the good news. We become fearful of other things without reason, waiting for a catastrophe that never arises.

This energy of fear needs expression to be freed. Talking about it takes its power away and is a good thing, but it never really goes away all the way.

The technique I share in the last part of this book is the way to be free of it.

Now imagine how many of such experiences we go through daily in our lives. We do nothing with those experiences because we don't know what to do with them. We bring the energies of all prior lifetimes that we have not yet healed into this lifetime. The energy of these experiences accumulates and results in dis-ease or discomfort to get our attention. Disease lets us know that trauma is not resolved.

Trauma does not know the difference of time passed. Trauma that remains unhealed in the family gets passed on. I have never had even a single client whose physical symptoms did not result from their past unresolved trauma.

Experiencing trauma is a pain in the butt, but we can choose to view it as a gift. The healing is hidden in the trauma when we begin to "see" what our soul wants us to see. To transcend the trauma is to heal the trauma. Can you imagine each new day of your life as a blank canvas? Then can you imagine your trauma as the brush and your experiences as all the colours of the rainbow? How would you hold the brush? Which colour would you use? How would you create each stroke? Can you see the blank canvas of your life transforming into a beautiful painting that you designed just the way you like it? Trauma breaks us open to reveal our resources, our strength, and our wholeness.

We come here to heal and evolve our souls. Everyone that has hurt or traumatized us in this life is part of our healing team. They are part of our soul contract to wake us up to our inner strength, resilience, and wholeness.

Our Soul's Blueprint

We must ride the energetic wave of what we have created in our personal soul blueprint in our past lives. Our patterns of behaviour serve our soul contracts.

Everything that we respond or react to negatively in life reflects the suffering and pain held within our personal blueprint, which is carried from one lifetime to the next. During our life, we have many opportunities to heal these energies, as they will continue to be mirrored in our life's experiences. Each time we ignore what is being mirrored to us, the energies will build momentum, often causing traumatic situations to reoccur to get our attention. These energies will be carried from one lifetime to another, and can often express themselves as physical pain, emotional ups and downs, and disease.

Not only that, we pass these energies on to our kids. I inherited many energetic patterns of the women in my lineage; understanding that was pivotal in my own healing so I don't pass them on to my kid. My mother did not know, but I know.

Our soul yearns to be free. So, it decides to create experiences for us so we can see the energy being played out in the hopes that this time we can free ourselves of the lower energies. The technique you will learn in this book is very effective in healing those energies.

There are No Victims

When I first started my Ayurveda practice, I felt overwhelmed by all the trauma stories of my clients. I felt their pain profoundly, and it kept me awake many nights. It got to the point that I had to talk to my mentor, Dr. Paul Dugliss; maybe I can't do this work, I told him. He explained it this way: When we pay the mortgage for our homes, with each installment, we feel financially free. When we experience pain in our life, our soul is rejoicing as it is becoming free of the old debt – karma. At our soul level, we have decided on our experiences in order to heal and grow. In this deeper understanding, there are no victims. This knowledge relieved my suffering about my clients and it relieved their suffering as well. Now, I know this deeply and am able to pass this on to my clients regardless of how traumatic their experiences may be. Knowing that they had agreed at the soul level to experience what they are experiencing empowers them. The question before them is why? This makes them want to learn the lessons sooner than later.

Nothing happens without our soul's permission, and our entire life is set up by our soul in our personal blueprint to learn the lessons and evolve. In that sense, there are no victims.

To heal our pain is to feel it deeply and to open our hearts to it. The feeling isn't fun and it's much easier to distract ourselves from the pain or to talk ourselves out of it. The experience, however, has already happened and becomes part of our subconscious mind. Living this way, we accumulate a lot of unprocessed experiences in our subconscious garbage bin that needs to be emptied out. Left unattended for a long time, it begins to empty into our habits and behaviours, and finally gets dumped on our bodies. This creates perpetual suffering. It's a dis-ease of the body/mind, and we call it disease as if it just appeared out of nowhere. The dis-ease has been happening for a long time.

Pushing unpleasant thoughts and feelings blocks our energy and creates even more burden on our subconscious, perpetuating our suffering.

Transformation is about freedom from suffering. As we continue to go deeper into healing the negative energies, all that we had held on to or had tucked away will begin to surface. Staying present and looking beyond the pain is part of the work.

This work is about taking personal responsibility for all we experience and bringing it into the full circle of Love. This is ultimate Self-Love. This is how we come full circle with our own darkness remembering that it is part of the light and becoming whole and Full-Spectrum Beings. Love includes everything that does not feel like love; light includes darkness. This is Holism; this is who we are; messy complex translations of our energies and all parts of us needs to be honoured.

Spiritual Bypassing

Spiritual bypassing is when we use spirituality to escape from painful experiences; being Love and Light when what we feel is quite different. Spiritual bypassing is something we made up without understanding what spirituality is. When we meditate to transcend all of our experiences without going through the process of healing them, we are spiritually bypassing.

This reminds me of a time when my son was very young. We went to get a Christmas tree, and the store was closed. All the trees were outside but there was no one there to take our payment. *"Looks like we will have to come back tomorrow," I said to my son. He had been wanting a tree all day and didn't want to wait anymore. "Mom, let's just take the tree, you can always put a Yoga spin on it so make it look like we didn't steal it", he suggested.*

Kids are funny. You've got to love them.

This may not be a great example, but spiritual bypassing is kind of like that, making something look different than it really is.

Spiritual bypassing is like window dressing our homes while the inside of the home is messy and dirty. Here we deny the reality of our experiences and hang on to the concept of Love and Light. Here, life feels like a figment of our imagination, not real. This is very confusing to our psyche. I have many clients who are on the path of Yoga and Spirituality, yet they don't understand why they feel so unhappy.

What is Spirituality? Spirituality is HOW we do everything; it's about penetrating the deep layers of our own psyche so there is more of our own self available to live and to create the life we desire and ultimately to be a beacon of love for those around us. We move toward becoming who we are designed to be - the Multidimensional Being, the Possible Human.

Spirituality is not separate from how we eat or interact with others. It's not about meditating our troubles away but instead infusing this remembering into every breath we take and into every moment we live.

When we think of spirituality, we often get images of light and people meditating away. This is how it can look from the outside, the inside work that is happening can be quite the opposite. The path to spirituality is often laden with grit and gruel, a never-ending process of feeling deeply, connecting the dots, and awakening. It's a container of the whole of our human life that holds all of our experiences. The truth is that there is nothing that is outside of spirituality; our mental and emotional challenges are not any less spiritual than our meditating, praying, or eating.

There is no bypassing in spirituality. It's something that our ego conjured up and created a mental shortcut. Spirituality is not a mental concept rather an experience of our being in this world.

The only way out of the suffering is to go through healing. When we push the pain away, we push it deep into our subconscious, like pushing something down with a lid hoping it won't blow;

this resistance to knowing what is inside creates enough pressure to blow the cover off. This is actually what happens when we blow up and create chaos around us.

We have all done that.

We are moving away from this way of living to a new way of living with a deep awareness of all of our experiences. We hold space for pain. We love our pain, we allow it to be there, we acknowledge and we accept it and then we open our hearts to it. This you will learn in the last part of this book.

Mastering Our Mind

Our mind is our greatest asset; it's because of the mind that we can exercise our superpowers. Or it can be our biggest liability, the weight of which our collective humanity is now buried under.

Mind is our enemy if we listen to it without integrating it with the Greater Knowing. The Greater Knowing is in the heart. Mind is our ego. Ego is needed; to have an ego is not shameful or less spiritual. it's the opposite. Ego gives us identification as to the roles we play in the world. For example, I may call myself a writer or an author; I use this identification to write this book. But to have the book flow through me, I also have to separate from it because I am not this book; I am not what I write; I am simply a conduit of what needs to be written so it can be available for all. If I live my entire life telling everyone that I am a writer and that they should also be a writer because it's so great to be a writer, I am now tying a noose around my own neck, limiting myself to being only a writer when I am so much more than that. This would be the result of my ego running amuck.

The mess that has shown up in the world is an example of our collective ego running amuck, undermining nature and the Greater Intelligence that rules and will continue to rule. Instead of understanding this Greater Power and bowing down to it, we are trying to control everything falsely believing we can. Realizing that something bigger must lead and allow our ego and mind to take a back seat and simply follow, we will heal. The world will become better because we have learned how to redirect the ego, and we have mastered our minds.

A mind is a tool and an asset if we learn to use it that way; left unattended, undirected and untrained, it is like a two-year-old left alone at home without potty training. The point is not to make the mind wrong, but rather to train it to operate through the heart. I like to call it Heart-Based Ego.

We have been in the mental flow, where the mind/ego has been in charge. Mind argues, complicates everything and resolves nothing. We will learn how to integrate the mind into the heart and train it to work through the heart.

Mind is important but it no longer leads in 5D consciousness.

The mind is used to getting caught up in the details of the story, a bookkeeping of who did what, and a mental understanding of the situation. The mind argues to keep the status quo, defends our old beliefs and that's how we keep falling into the grooves of our old conditioning. We are here to heal, not to win a debate on who is right and wrong.

The Six Aspects of Our Being

In the ancient traditions and wisdom, the heart is viewed as a Six-Pointed-Star. All that needs healing is held in our six aspects; our Higher Self, Mental Body, Emotional Body, Physical Body, Spirit Body, and Soul.

When the mind is operating through the heart, all of our six aspects are harmonized, and the heart becomes the Six-Pointed Star, what it was designed for.

Once all these aspects work in harmony as a single unit, we experience love's wholeness. With each lifetime, we shut down a little more. The 6A Technique that you are about to learn can heal all aspects of our being and uplift us into the 5th Dimensional Being that we are created to be.

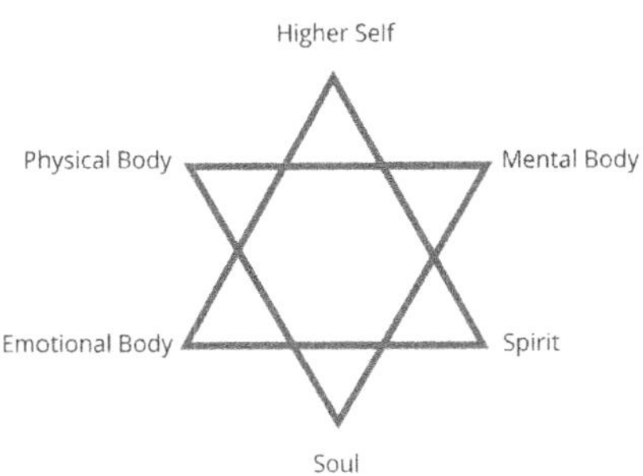

Part III

The Six Steps: The 6A Technique

The 6A Technique

The six steps to emotional freedom are the 6A technique.

The 6A technique is a simple yet powerful method for transmuting the lower energies and can assist us in healing all of our stored-up pain and suffering and free us. This technique, when practiced regularly, can move mountains of energy and is a foundational process in assisting the dark negative energies to expand into the Full Spectrum of Love.

This Full Spectrum of Love includes not only the love, joy, and happiness in life but also the pain, fear, and anger that we have created in our soul's journey. This perception of Love sees all life as being a part of Love. With our willingness to fully accept life just as it is, all is transformed and expanded into a Full Spectrum of Love. This allows us to have the wisdom and understanding of what we have gained from the pain and suffering and enables us to live as Full Spectrum Beings of Pure Love, loving and honouring all life without exception.

This fulfils our purpose in life to be a clear and open channel for the Heavens to flow their Love through us, anchoring Heaven on Earth so that all life on this planet may live in a Love-based realm. Each of us is a key player in the gradual shift from a fear-based to a Love-based realm. This simple technique will allow you to experience this shift within yourself so that you may live as a Fifth Dimensional expression of Humanity and as a being of Pure Love.

Here is a summary of this technique, and the details will follow. Each step is not independent of the other rather it's a part of the whole process. Our inner psychological world is complex, and everything affects everything else, so we are always going back and forth in this technique to gain clarity and heal. We practice this technique in our hearts so we can embody the transformation.

1. Awareness: Becoming aware of what is taking place and how we participate in every situation in our lives.

2. Allowance: We open our hearts to all we are becoming aware of and allow the awareness to continue and let the Love flow.

3. Acceptance: We take radical personal responsibility for all of our experiences, without the need to change or hide anything and letting go of all judgement.

4. Appreciation: As we accept these energies, the heart will naturally open to feel appreciation for everything these energies have shown us.

5. Application: When we apply this technique in our lives, we bring this work into reality; we live it and be it. This is how we get all of our suffering and pain to a "Full Circle of Love" to set ourselves free!

6. Anchoring: By continuously applying this technique, we anchor into our hearts. This is how we anchor Heaven on Earth and it brings our entire life's journey to a 'Full Circle of Love' within us, which allows the Heavens to flow their Love and Light freely through us, fulfilling our purpose in life.

This process is actually happening in our world. The awareness is rising, we are acknowledging the mess we are in and realizing that we have created it. Our world is waking up. Many are realizing the gift of these times. We are headed to the other side of darkness.

The First A: Awareness

Awareness is the first and the most important step in healing. It takes our awareness to know that something is off track.

When we realize we are reacting negatively to a situation, we have the choice to open ourselves and become aware of what is taking place and our participation in this situation. The work here is to become conscious of our feelings and notice when they are not of Love; that's the time to process these energies with this technique.

Most of us move about our day in 'oblivious awareness', not conscious of what is going on, just moving from one thing to the next, not fully aware of all that is taking place in our lives. This 'oblivious awareness' shuts us down to life.

We don't heal trauma if we don't know it is there. We have formed many habits and patterns living in a fear-based realm and progressively shutting down to Love. Now it will take deep awareness to open the doorway to our freedom.

When we ask for assistance from the Heavens, our Guardians or Angels to keep expanding to greater awareness of what life is presenting to us, we will find ourselves being more aware and present in life. The Heavens will help us in every way they can; however, they cannot take these energies from us; we own these energies and they are a part of our being. It takes our free will choice to be aware and open our hearts to these energies and allow them to expand in Love. As we participate in the process of becoming a fully Conscious Being, fully aware and present with all life, we begin to see more and more of all life as a part of Love.

The more we practice awareness in our life, the more our awareness will expand.

Awareness is the foundational stone of this process and the key to making immeasurable changes in our life. Become aware of how we participate in life; are we flowing with it, or are we controlling it? If you find yourself controlling life, there is no need to judge yourself as it will only add to your resistance. Simply become aware of it.

Awareness is about expanding the field of our seeing and knowing. It is painful in the beginning, like taking the bandage off, but the wounds heal with time as we air them out. When we tune into how we feel, that which needs more awareness will naturally rise to the surface.

Like using a magnifying glass, you can allow your awareness to expand with these questions; 1. What is the experience? Can you name it?
2. Why is it there? 3. What's behind it? 4. How is it affecting my life?
5. Does it continue to repeat in my life? 6. Expand sensory awareness by asking: what does it taste, smell, and feel like? Who is present, what's the colour of the surroundings etc.?

You are going inside this awareness to uncover all that is there for you. It will feel like it is happening right now. Our subconscious does not keep track of the time passed; the energies simply sit there until we are ready to address them. This will bring the "what is" in fuller view, and it will expand your awareness of it.

The expanded awareness will show you where healing needs to take place. That which brings pain, suffering, darkness, and negativity is ready to be brought to love and healing.

Awareness is about seeing "what is" deeply without judgement, fear, and resistance, much like watching the waves on the ocean from the beach. This can be a process as the resistance will surface. We simply become aware of that. Just trust that what’s rising to your awareness is what you are ready to address.

Continue to live in expanded awareness from moment to moment. Familiarize yourself deeply with the feeling level of your experiences and get to know yourself deeper.

Activating Your Senses

Our sensory awareness can bring forth a lot of information that we may not otherwise know. I always like to include sensory activation with my clients as it heightens their knowing and seeing. In one of Dr. Jean Houston's lectures, I learned a few examples she used in activating the senses and I am sharing them here with you. Some examples to work with are 1. Chew an apple in your mind. Feel the juice running in between your teeth. Taste the sweetness. 2. Have a salad of wild greens with the hint of almond oil and lemon. 3. Feel the soft nose of a kitten. 4. Plunge both hands into a bowl of potato chips and break them all, then lick the salty fingers. 5. Climb a tree and feel the warm rough bark under your feet. Bringing the specific texture or taste can help us in our imagination and wake up our sensory perception.

During the awareness part of the 6A technique, there is no limit to what can show up. What shows up results from what you have experienced in your life and what you have stored away. Many emotions can arise that can catch us off guard and surprise us. This is perfect as it's precisely these emotions blocking the path of our healing. Remember, emotions always arise for self-examination and self-purification; they are not meant to burn others, and that's exactly what happens if we don't take the time to examine them.

Here is my perspective on some of the most common emotions that can arise to help you guide through them:

Anger

One of the most common emotions we all experience is anger. Anger is a great disguiser and a great mobilizer. Let me explain. When we don't check in with ourselves and tune into how we feel, these experiences continue to accumulate in the subconscious. Minor irritations, a bit of guilt, a bit of feeling bad, a bit of this, and a bit of that can turn into intense feelings leaving us wondering why we are feeling the way we are. Left unaddressed, this can turn into a big blow-up in conversations and catches everyone by surprise. Eventually, every emotion unexpressed turns into anger or rather hides under it. In other words, anger is just the tip of the iceberg.

Hence the importance of tuning into yourself, centering, and checking in with yourself. To become even more aware is to name the emotion you are feeling. Asking yourself the cause of your anger will begin to uncover the emotions that are hiding under it.

Anger is needed to move energy when we become stagnant. The anger we are experiencing in the external world is uncovering the pent-up emotions that we have come to heal.

Emotions are energy in motion that seek expression. To feel the anger is a way to start expressing the anger and to mobilize other emotions that are hiding beneath it. Energy is in the body, so using the body in expressing anger is highly useful. How do you express anger?

My client took her dishes out to the garage, and, one by one, smashed them on the floor, breaking them; her anger unleashed as she smashed each dish to the floor with great intensity. She then collected the pieces and made a beautiful mosaic out of them. This step started her healing process.

We can throw punches in the air, we can scream (close the doors and windows) and make up curse words, kick a ball; the object of our anger does not need to be there, and it should not be there. We don't need to scream at somebody or hurt someone, we simply need to express it within ourselves. We have been conditioned to suppress anger, so we have learned to pretend it away and put on a smiley face. This way of being can't serve us in the New World. Anger is real. We want to use anger as a tool and not as a weapon.

We must allow ourselves to express anger in healthy ways otherwise it will show up in unhealthy ways as it often does.

Fear

What's beneath anger many times is fear; fear of being judged, ridiculed, isolated, abandoned, fear of the unknown, fear of not being enough, fear of being found out. I like to contend that underneath all emotions is fear. Guilt, shame, and blame all join in. Suppose we genuinely don't want to visit our mother because she judges everything we do, so we don't go. We are afraid of being judged. Alongside fear, now guilt, shame, and blame (it's her fault that we don't want to go etc.) show up for not going.

Guilt is made up by the mind because you did not do as you should. Anytime we use the words "should" or "could", we are working with old programming or conditioning. There is never a happy ending when we operate out of conditioning. The truth is that the heart is actually quite content being in peace and not going. Mind says you are bad for not going. What to do? We don't go, but we hold the guilt. Underneath all of it is anger about being judged. Guilt results from fear of owning or claiming our truth. We can simply tell her how we feel. But no one does that, "oh I don't want to hurt her feelings, she will get mad, she will never understand, etc." This is a dilemma we create for ourselves. This is just an example of how complex and convoluted our inner psyche can be.

Guilt is our mental way of avoiding punishment by others for not following the status quo. Guilt fills the gap between what is and what our conditioned self believes it should be. So as long as I carry a little guilt with me, I will do what I want to do. What I truly want to do = what I should do + guilt. Shame and blame follow and make this lower energetic trinity in all of us.

Guilt, shame, blame are constructs of the mind to make us feel we “fit in” so we can be spared the criticisms and judgments. These experiences take away our sovereignty. Choose them if you are looking to fit in, otherwise, look deeper!

We can truly do what we want to do. Guilt does not need to be part of the equation. This is our 5D way of living.

“What do you truly want and need” is a question worth asking yourself again and again. The truth is when we lead from our heart, no one gets hurt. It’s the mind that wants to keep the inner and outer drama alive.

For the purposes of this process, continue to be aware of what it is that you are feeling and allow it.

You will learn in the following chapters that fear by itself is not a thing. Fear is a lack of Love. Love is the real emotion. Loving our fear is the work to ease our guilt and to stop the anger before it festers.

Fear is of the unknown and the mind/ego imagines the worst, which limits the flow. The unknown can either take us to fear or the magical place within ourselves where all is possible. Drop into the heart to really "know" the unknown, where all is possible. Let the unknown be a catalyst to connect to the field of all possibilities.

Let the unknown help you cultivate trust.

Self-Worth

We were born into the culture of shame and worthlessness with the belief that inherently we are all broken. We spend our lifetime "fixing" ourselves to no avail. Trying to find our self-worth with outer accomplishments is like chasing our tail because we are looking in the wrong direction.

Worth is God-given! Our human life is evidence enough that we are worthy; worthy of evolving and healing through our human life. Our worth is independent of others' opinions, our accomplishments, our social and financial status, race and culture, and abilities or disabilities. Do we believe our Creator is worthy? How then can we not be worthy?

In 5D Consciousness, we are whole and we are enough. When we pivot from this place, everything we do turns beautiful and so does the world around us. Since the outer world only mirrors our inner world, we may experience our wholeness, our worth, and our beauty in all of our experiences.

When we truly believe in our self-worth, we lose interest in proving it. We simply live from wholeness. We believe others are whole. Judgement is no longer part of our vocabulary, fear disappears, we simply and naturally live in our Divinity.

The Second A: Allowance

Becoming aware of some things within ourselves can be unpleasant and painful. Here the ego interferes by pretending that we don't know what we know. The work is to notice that and allow the awareness to be there. Allowance is easy when we acknowledge what we have become aware of. For example, acknowledging that I am angry most of the time is allowing myself to feel the anger. Here we can hold curiosity and see what unfolds.

The ego's job is to challenge us tooth and nail to maintain the status quo. We have to sometimes arm wrestle with our ego.

Allowing is about consciously opening our hearts to our own reactions and allowing Love to flow with them. It's about keeping our hearts open to the 'what is' of life at that moment. In the beginning, you may feel there is nothing or nothing to be aware of. Be patient, it will show up. We have to remember that we have been shut down to the vastness of who we are and this process is assisting us to open and expand in

Love, allowing us to be the Divine Being that is deep inside us; it is a process of awakening and becoming whole once again!

Awareness without acknowledgment creates inner conflict and psychological complexities. Acknowledging is validating how we feel; it's like a breath of fresh air that takes away the need to suppress our feelings for the fear of expressing them.

The Third A: Acceptance

We begin the 6A process in the heart with awareness. Because we are in our heart, right from the start, love is flowing with the whole process. As you keep allowing Love to flow with these energies, you will automatically flow right into acceptance. As you accept these energies just as they are, allowing them to flow through your heart in complete acceptance without the need to change them, hide them, categorize them or judge them in any way, you will free them.

Each one of these energies has a spark of Love within it, and they are all a part of you. With your full acceptance of these energies, the spark will expand into a full flame of Love in your heart, and become a Full Spectrum of Love in your Matrix.

Awareness, Allowance, and Acceptance, also called "The Triple-A" all work together and are foundational for transmuting lower energies.

Key in this step is accepting darkness, our journey, and what we have been through and opening our hearts to it. Fear is at the base of the resistance.

Accepting darkness as part of love is what will open the flow. It is a new way, the new realm. We are participating, and we don't shut down to life; we don't shut down to fear and keep the love flowing. This is Full Spectrum. Gradually more love begins to show itself in our life.

Acceptance is about taking radical personal responsibility. It's not about what they did to you, rather it's about what you experienced. This is where our power is; taking responsibility for our own experiences.

We fear that if we accept something, we have to live with it for the rest of our lives. It's the opposite. Once we accept, it no longer holds power over us, and secondly so much of our energy that was vested in denying "what is" gets freed up for solutions. Acceptance is the key to bringing about change.

Resisting adds momentum to what we are resisting.

Acceptance is not complacency. Accepting something does not mean we like it or agree with it; It means we are no longer willing to waste our precious energy resisting what is. Acceptance also does not mean we don't do all we can do to change our lives. We show up for our life and for what is important to us. We let go of the attachment to the results. Life will continue to mirror all we are and all that is ready to know love. Continuing to drop into the heart and expanding it with the One Flow of Love is how to heal all that life has presented. This is how we open the flood gates of change.

At the soul level, we have agreed to heal these energies, and that's why we are experiencing them. When we heal, we are healing the pain of our ancestors.

When we accept others even when they are shut down, they can experience love within themselves and slowly open to more love. We can accept others as God having a human experience.

If we can't see God in all, we can't see God at all.

Acceptance breaks down the wall that separates us from love; instead of fixing, we are accepting. This stops the cycle of pain. We don't get rid of anything; we simply open our hearts to that part of ourselves we have been resisting.

Acceptance of darkness brings us freedom from the darkness as it has God flow in it; it is inclusive and sparkling. When we draw a line in the sand, we block the flow of love and feel unworthy of receiving it. When we accept Love in its wholeness, we become it. When we accept, we are okay with whatever life shows up and trust in the unknown. A lot shows up in this process. So, it can take some time to fully accept the "what is. We just work at the layer that shows up.

Let's talk about a few things that may show up in the process of acceptance:

Judgement

We judge in others what we are not yet willing to acknowledge within ourselves. Somewhere along our journey, we have judged ourselves for the same reasons we are now judging others. The others mirror and therefore provide an opportunity to see this within us and bring it to wholeness. The other person is you. Judgement is part of acceptance, holistic acceptance.

What we judge is who we are and/or will become.

There is no one good or bad, nothing right or wrong, only the experiences of these energies. It's only the mind's need to judge something or someone as good and bad. Judging something or someone creates the energy that cycles back to the one judging.

Judgement is part of wholeness, so we don't need to judge the judgments. Simply allowing Love to flow with our judgement is how to transmute it to a higher frequency of Love Unified. Ironically, when we begin to value ourselves fully without judgement, we also let go of judging others.

Trust

Acceptance requires that we let go of what we want for now and fully accept what is. This can surface fear in a big way. This is where we cultivate trust. Trust will bring what we need, and it may be way beyond what we can imagine in our limited thinking. Worry, anxiety, and mistrust are part of it and the work is to flow Love with it.

The unknown is beyond any limitations and has all that we need. Trusting it opens the floodgates to all that is available to us. Trusting in Divine timing and process is the ultimate surrender.

The process of 6A technique is to pull in all the opposites and weave all of our life's experiences like a tapestry. Everything needs everything for it to be whole. There is nothing to defend from when we merge everything into the One.

Worry is imaginary, and it does not have to manifest. Whatever is surfacing in our world is on its way out. We don't kick anything out; fear, darkness, and resistance is the other side of Love. We have been accustomed to one-sided love and bypass the darker side of love. It is now time to expand the definition of Love and understand and experience it as Full Spectrum Love.

We continue the process, and it becomes a new way of handling negativity, pain, or conflict in our lives. This way of dealing with life's ups and downs will expand us into wholeness. We remind the ego gently that we are beginning to deal with things differently.

This work may feel hard initially because we have been used to bypassing the darker experiences. This work is about going through the process of transforming them.

Resistance

Well-being is our natural state, and life always seeks to return us to it. What hampers well-being is not some external factor but internal resistance. All pain, physical, emotional, or spiritual, begins and is maintained by a factor of "pushing against." When you release your resistance, healing rushes in. Life wants us to be healed and constantly moves to accomplish that; it simply awaits our cooperation. To be healed physically, emotionally, mentally, or spiritually, we don't have to make anything happen, but to just let go of what we are resisting.

Whenever we are reactive, we are not free; we strengthen whatever we resist. Expectation and disappointment are portable prisons for us and for others. "Willingness is the dance partner of life", as my teacher, Cassandra, would say. To be willing is to be the liberator.

Now, to end the pain of past trauma, we must free the energy. When we resist the pain, we are resisting or creating a wall between ourselves and the energy of that experience. That creates resistance which gives this energy more power. Temporarily, we may feel the relief, but the experience repeats; the story may change but each new similar experience becomes more intense as it is now powered by the past experiences, rather past energies that we have yet to free.

This is where we examine the narrative that we have instilled into our psyche. How long have you been putting up with pain or a situation that is not working? How long have you not had use of a part of your life that you would rather enjoy? What do you think needs to happen before you can feel good? If we believe something in the outside world needs to change before we feel good, then we delay the process and it's also one of the ways we resist.

Resistance is part of the process, the fact that you are resisting is showing that you are resisting something – that something is the inkling within you nudging you, telling you that you can feel better and heal the past. Fear of feeling the pain of revisiting the past or fear of becoming a healed version of you can be scary and is part of the resistance. Just keep moving through it. Your process has already started. Just get out of the way. When we no longer use our energy in fighting with what we feel, we spare that much more energy for our wellbeing. We raise the bar on the quality of our life. It is no longer a mediocre life; it is a life of high vibration where we do things we never thought possible

As our inner life evolves, what matters more and more is how we are being with whatever life brings us. We acknowledge and accept that the outcome is ultimately beyond our control.

Resistance represents our deep desire to heal. Resistance will show up as strongly as our desire to heal and fear is one of the ways that resistance shows up. Our natural response to that resistance is to take it at its face value and stop the process. Instead, we can view it as a sign that healing has begun.

By resisting, we give more power to the energies behind our conditioned patterns, and we continue to repeat these patterns. No amount of willpower is enough to stop the energies of these patterns, they continue to recycle. We must free the energies of them in our hearts. The work is to take full responsibility for these energies and open our hearts to them so they can be freed in Love. That's how we gain freedom from the patterns.

For example, if you feel abandoned, chances are it's not the first time. If you feel worthless, this is what you have felt before. Talking ourselves out of feeling what we feel makes the energy of it even stronger and it is that energy which continues to recycle in our psyche over and over again. That's why talk therapy alone does not work because the energy is in the body, it must be freed from the body. When we drop into our hearts, we are in the body.

As you continue to work with this process, you may even get a sense that there are two separate energies flowing into your heart, one is open and flowing and the other is restrictive, which could include pain or resistance. Allow them to flow together as you bring them into your heart, not judging them or changing them in any way and letting go of all resistance to them.

If at first, you don't feel these energies, try to imagine them flowing into your heart. The old saying, 'fake it until you make it,' applies here. Your open-hearted acceptance of the energies flowing at that moment, just as they are, will allow the energies to transform into a greater expression of Love. They will gradually flow together and become ONE Flow of Love, combining the two energies into what is called a Full Spectrum of Love which includes the suffering and the pain as well as joy and happiness in life, creating the ecstatic feelings of Love that embraces all life. This meaning of Love does not deny or resist any part of life, as fear becomes your ally when you embrace it with Love and allow it to expand.

Radical Responsibility

Our power is in taking radical responsibility for all we experience. We tend to focus on the details of the story and on what others did to us; this distracts us from our own experiences and how we have contributed energetically in creating our own experiences. Remember that all memory is flawed as we haven't looked at our participation in our experiences. What we remember is what serves and solidifies our beliefs; this not only distorts our story but also keeps us stuck in it.

Let this be your mantra: I am the KEY to set myself free!

We affect others and are affected by others energetically. We are part of collective energy and the whole of Creation. Our mind is part of the Universal Mind, so we pick up thoughts/feelings or rather their energy; hence the explanation behind how many people are thinking the same thing in a day, a meeting, or in a seminar. On a lighter note, "we can run, but we can't hide" is so true. People around us can read our thoughts, and we can read theirs.

We are all working with the energies that we brought from prior lifetimes. We are living these energies out so we can see them in order to heal them. Our soul chose these life experiences to heal, but we forget and get stuck in the suffering.

All that is painful in our lives is ready to know Love. When we step into our own heart, we step into the heart of the Creator. We connect with the vast, endless source of Love that continues to expand within ourselves. This changes our inner experiences, and our outside life now begins to mirror that change.

We have been accustomed to one-sided love and we have bypassed the darker side of love. It is now time to expand the definition of Love and understand and experience Love as Full Spectrum Love. We don't kick anything out; fear, darkness, resistance is the other side of Love.

Forgiveness

When we don't forgive another person, we have stolen their soul and remain connected. The greatest cause of burnout is soul-stealing. We can steal the soul but can't use it. It's used energy that is burdening you. You must release it and be free of it. Soul stealing is cursing. On the other hand, no one can steal your soul unless you let them. We have free will and choice.

Forgiveness is not ours to do! Who are we to forgive others? We are neither the judge nor the jury of anyone. No one does anything to us without our permission; everything we do is between us and our Higher Self.

The only person we need to forgive is ourselves.

The Fourth A: Appreciation

Appreciation is about seeing our challenges as a gift. The real gift is finally "waking up" and "seeing" the miracle our life really is. It's not gratitude. It's about recognizing the value of our challenges even when we don't feel grateful. It's asking the question as to who you are because of your challenges rather than the pain you endured from them.

What challenge in your life took you to the next level of your growth and evolution?

As you continue to work with this technique, your heart will naturally open to feel appreciation for everything these energies have shown you. Once you have fully accepted them, you will open your heart to feel a celebration for life where you are dancing for no reason, happy like a child, and appreciating yourself and life for the gifts that have been given to you. You will feel appreciation for all your aspects for their courage and their willingness to keep showing up. Embrace the pain of your experiences with love, be vulnerable and invite the energies forward. This will merge them into love within you. You will experience yourself becoming freer and freer as you allow your whole being to expand in Love, accepting your life just as it is. Appreciation becomes a natural flow of acknowledging and celebrating your life as Love.

Can you see how each challenge or difficulty brought you closer to your true essence? This is the point of life, of our challenges in life, to take us home to ourselves.

Appreciation is an important step in the process of transmuting energies, and it is very easy to skip it. However, it is important to keep working with the energies all the way through to appreciation, so that you can experience the joy and celebrate these energies and your life journey.

The Fifth A: Application

By applying the previous 4A's, we embody these teachings, create Heaven on Earth and make it a reality. This is also where we can get pulled into the same old way of reacting, judging, and trying to resolve our experiences mentally rather than in the body. It's just like changing any habit. First, become aware of what's happening in the mind and then take a pause to drop into the heart and apply the 4A's; each time you try this technique, the energies will be freer and freer and you will feel lighter and lighter.

Application is a very important part of this process because if you are not applying it in your life, you have not brought the suffering and pain to a "Full Circle of Love" to set yourself free. The application of this process is surrendering life to that which is greater.

Look for opportunities where you can try this technique; at work, at home, with friends, with the news. We are given endless opportunities to use this technique, especially during this time. And that's exactly what's needed to transmute the current negative energies. Notice how you feel when you try this technique rather than when you try to resolve it mentally. The experience of using this technique feels so much better, calmer, and fuller and it is this experience that will remind you to use it again and again. In so doing, your unpleasant experiences will be far and wide and this is how you begin to bring peace in your life and into the life of those around you.

It's in the application of the 4A's that knowledge transforms into wisdom. We can easily fall back into our old way of being, complaining, or rehashing the pain of the past. This is exactly where we need to clue in; we know more, we now know a different way, and this is where we drop into the heart and go through the 6A technique.

Be patient, kind, and gentle, and slowly this will become your new habit. In the process, you'll get to experience both ways of being and your Higher Self will choose the one that feels better and feels like home.

You live the teachings and participate fully in life. You begin to recognize that you are Love and you allow your true self to blossom. You bring duality into Unity with every conscious choice you make.

This technique cultivates Unity Consciousness for it holds space for the whole of life.

When you find yourself moving into duality, there is no need to judge yourself, just expand Love into this dual way of thinking until it becomes so immersed in Love that it becomes a greater expression of Love. This is what is being asked of each one of us, to be an example of a being of Pure Love that accepts all life as part of Love, without exception.

The Fifth Dimension is the first step in living in a Love-based Realm, where you automatically choose Love, without excluding fear. This Love-based Realm that you are creating through your being will continue to grow until all of life can expand in Love. For the Heavens to flow through you in this unrestricted way it requires you to open to all of life and see it all as a part of Love.

Here we kick nothing out; fear, darkness, resistance is all part of Love, it's just the other side of it that we have not wanted to see. It's now time to expand the definition of Love and understand it to be a Full Spectrum love. There is either Love or lack of. All darker emotions are lack of Love; to heal them is to show them Love. The task is to Love our pain. The work is to free the darkness into our own heart, so it can merge with the One Flow of Love.

The Sixth A: Anchoring

The last A in the 6A technique is anchoring; anchoring our life in Love and living from a place of Love. Here we are in the heart, and our mind is in service to our heart. Heart leads, mind follows. Heart knows, in that knowing is the Higher thinking, much superior than the limited ego-based thinking. Here, we love the self that judges, love our inner critic; we love all the neglected and abandoned parts of ourselves, becoming more and more whole with each experience. Here, there is simply no room for should or could. We soften. There is no need to draw a line in the sand or use ultimatums. Heavens don't judge us and neither do we.

This is how we anchor Heaven on Earth. This is where we bring our entire life's journey within us so the Heavens can flow their Love and Light freely through us. We become a conduit, a beacon of Love. This is the supreme alignment with the Source.

Continuously applying the 6A technique is how we anchor in Love.

What is Love

Love is the most elusive, most used and most wanted experience. We wait for it; to be in Love, to be loved, to feel love. We chase it and seldom experience it.

Again, it's a matter of changing direction. The direction is inwards. Love is who and what we are at the core of our being. It may feel like a vague concept because it can only be understood by experiencing it and most importantly, it must be realized within ourselves. How can we experience Love when all of our life's experiences are far removed from it? That's why we do this work. With this work, we understand how to love our pain. In so doing, we cultivate our heart – the reservoir of this Love Energy.

We are more familiar with Love in the romantic sense; falling in love and falling out of love. The mere idea of "falling" implies the end of all consciousness; the symptoms many times are that of depression: lack of sleep, hunger, euphoria, being in the clouds; obsession, a preoccupation, escape, a fantasy. All of our unmet needs are surfaced, and we fool ourselves by thinking that this person will fulfil all of our dreams. We get re-wounded. We have ideas of what it should be; it's like trying to fit a square into a circle. This causes heartache, and we mistake it for "being in love."

Without a direct experience of Love, we make up all kinds of notions about it and become a prisoner of our own fantasies and thoughts; "If you love me, then you will do this." The love we are used to is love without Consciousness. This kind of love leads to control, fear and manipulation as we often experience in our relationships.

We think love is a feeling, which implies it can change as all feelings change. So, we keep chasing the feeling, and further away it gets. Then, we go to the feelings that "feel like love," and we come to the feelings of peace, fulfilment, balance, happiness, joy, kindness, freedom, compassion, etc.

We begin to believe that love is everything positive, good, and nice. What about fear, pain, disappointment, confusion, judgment, hatred, anger, resentment, control, anxiety, humiliation, shame, blame, guilt, discrimination, manipulation, isolation, separation, put-downs, betrayals, broken hearts, deception, and all of our 3D experiences? Where do we put all of this and what do we do with it? So, what do we do? We keep reliving it in our heads recreating the same feelings and we can't help but pass it on to others. Energy can't be contained, it leaks out. This is how we perpetuate misery because we simply don't know what to do with it.

We put all of this in our hearts. How? By opening our hearts to our pain and misery. If we don't put it in our heart, it embeds it in our tissues, our organs, and will eventually show up as a disease. In our heart we feel our feelings and become free of them.

The new definition of Love includes all the experiences that don't feel like love. Instead of storing them in the body, we put them in the One Flow of Love, in our hearts. In the allowance and inclusion, resistance turns into acceptance; instead of feeling a victim of our experiences, we begin to appreciate them. Fear transforms into Love; anger reveals the pain of not being loved. Feeling the pain turns it into love, self-hatred turns to self-care, judgement transforms into acceptance, shame into vulnerability, guilt into self-love, lack into abundance, worry and anxiety into trust. Love becomes whole and not fragmented; then there is nothing that is not Love.

Love is a state of Consciousness. It is a constant and does not fluctuate. Love is the basis on which the entire Creation is resting. This field of Consciousness holds the trinity of Body, Mind, and Spirit. It's the seed of everything and nothing. All of our experiences arise out of this field.

How will your life experiences change if you shift into this all-inclusive broader perspective and understanding of Love?

In Love, all energies are free. Instead of seeking freedom from pain, we free the pain in Love. Love provides the greatest freedom from pain. Here the experience is like coming home to oneself and becoming one with our Truth. So much of our negative emotions arise in search of love and feeling abandoned by it. When we flow them in The One Flow of Love, the search is over. In this understanding, we don't fall in or fall out of love; we are Love. We rest when we come home to it.

This is our truth: Love and Light. It's not a fluffy, new-age concept; it's our reality.

This work is not about focusing on the positive or just being positive rather it's about understanding what to do with all that is not positive. Love becomes our pivot; it becomes our anchor.

Here, we live as a Being of Love instead of a "doing" of life.

Love is the energy of the highest vibration. All other lower energies seek to merge with this high energy. When we are fearful, reassurance that all will be okay dissipates our fear. When we feel hurt, kindness and compassion soothe our wounds. When we understand that, we begin to cultivate our own heart by opening it and we begin to flow love with our fears, we flow love to our wounds; this way realizing that Love was within us all along. We fill ourselves with Love, we become Love, we radiate Love.

We don't wait for someone to love us; all of us are wounded, one wounded person looking for love from another wounded person creates quite the crazy chase. We chase our desires into our own hearts, for we know they will be fulfilled there. Here, Love is the energy we naturally emit and fill our surroundings and our environment with it.

In understanding the history of humanity, the most important thing to remember is that we are anchored and created in Love and healing will take place when we solidify our connection with that knowing.

How to Open your Heart

Take a moment to do this exercise:

Drop into your heart and think of a person or a pet that you love deeply. Keep thinking of them and keep opening your heart to them. Notice how you feel. Some people begin to tear up, they soften, feel warm and they feel the expansion in their heart. How do you feel?

Now bring to your mind someone you can't stand. We all have at least one person in our life like that. Open your heart to them. Exactly. *One client said: Are you crazy? I can't open my heart to this person.* Notice how that feels. Do you feel constricted, bad, or tight? Do all of your feelings about this person surface? By contrast, not being able to open your heart is how you will know the feeling of opening your heart.

By bringing the mind into the heart, we are training it to operate from the heart.

Let's work with fear. Bring the part of you that is fearful into your heart and open your heart to the fearful you. Keep expanding and opening your heart so the fearful part of you is enveloped in this heart energy and when you keep doing that, it all becomes love. Now Love is expanded because it has fear in it. But fear is nowhere to be felt. This is how you transform your fears into Love. This is how Love heals. By this practice, you also train yourself in the subtle perception of how it feels when the heart is open vs when it is not.

To heal the pain is to love the pain. When we push the pain away, we are wanting to be free from it. But we can never destroy the energy because it's the law of energy. What we don't realize is that what we truly desire is to free this energy into Love. Love is where the energy of pain is freed.

We feel love by experiencing kindness, trust, compassion, and joy to name a few. These experiences arise out of a state of Consciousness or state of Love. Love is a state of Being, and it's the highest and the most creative power we have as humans. To know this Love is to cultivate our heart by continuously opening our heart to all of life. When Love is what we feel, it naturally flows out to others.

The need for love is met by giving it.

We can intentionally drop into our heart frequently throughout our day. This is how we connect with our heart and cultivate it for its potential. Choosing Love in every moment and holding on to all parts of ourselves is how we cultivate Love. Think of the heart as a filter that softens everything. Being in the mental flow, we become rigid, tense, and tunnel-visioned. The heart expands our vision; it softens us and helps us release unnecessary tension. The heart is our window to Pure Consciousness, to the Quantum field of all possibilities.

We are conditioned to think we always have to feel something, but when we are just being, the feeling is of ease, of balance, and alignment and we just go about our day peacefully without highs and lows and this is how we can be. This happens in expanded awareness, but we are not aware of the awareness as we become the awareness itself.

When we feel nothing, we are simply at ease, in flow, and are able to effortlessly go about our day. We are free.

Right/wrong is the mental flow; heart flow is as-is. The intention is to keep expanding with joy, freedom, playfulness, greater freedom, unity, and merge with the Heavens. From feeling shattered to the whole is how we heal the pain of separation.

It is our conscious choice to choose freedom, and the Heavens are giving us the keys to achieving our freedom in ways that honour all life. It is up to us to turn the Keys to open the doorways to the flow of Love, prosperity, and true freedom in our life.

The New Model for the Six-Pointed-Star

With the practice of the 6A Technique for transmuting energies, weaving all six of the A's together in our life, we can open every doorway to achieving our mastery. We can open to the unlimited flow of abundance and prosperity, more than we can imagine, living in Pure Consciousness as a full Spectrum Being of Love that honours and accepts all life which fulfils our Purpose in Life. It is a fantastic journey to experience life in this way. It is true FREEDOM!

It is what our collective humanity has been waiting for, and now is the time to say 'Yes!" and walk through the Doorway of Freedom!

The 6 A's form the new model for the Six-Pointed-Star.

The New Model for the Six-Pointed-Star

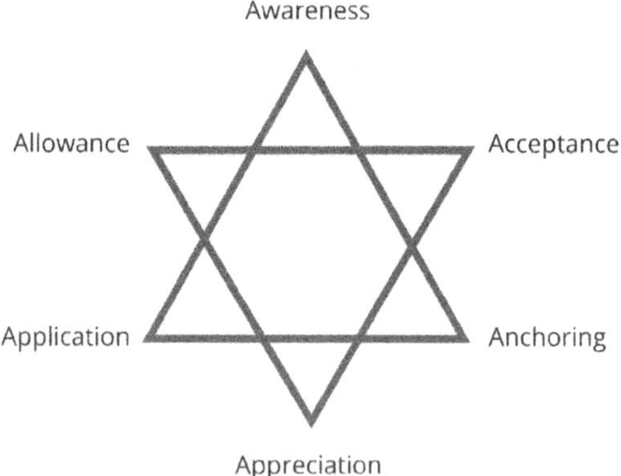

My Final Thoughts

When we stay in the dark, our eyes adjust, and we begin to see things. When we make a commitment to healing, all that needs our seeing will emerge slowly, we must stay with the process.

The world can either be a very hostile place or a beautiful place because of the people in it. We are the people. We have the power to either make the world a beautiful place or a horrible place. Why don't we use our power to make it a beautiful place? And we can only do it via our relationships with other fellow beings. The 6A Technique is an effective tool in creating amazing relationships with others.

Let Your Heart be the most important person in your life. Give it the support it deserves. Living in the 3D world, we had no contact with our heart. The heart is the currency of the future. Get deeply in touch with your heart currency; it's your future.

Eventually, we don't need any religion. It is all about Love. This is part of our journey, our history.

Love can heal seven million years of history and journey. Our Beingness was created so we could access the history, the very root of it. Step more and more in your wholeness; work deeper with Divine masculine (mental flow) and feminine (heart flow) to merge more with the Higher Self.

Love is the Ultimate Path to Emotional Freedom

What's Your Next Step?

Did this book speak to you?

Are you ready to do the deep inner work to create your world of Love, Peace, and Harmony?

To apply the learning in your life can be difficult and overwhelming. This work is about being the truer version of ourselves. We don't become ourselves by ourselves. Having support and guidance makes all the difference.

When you are ready for guidance, I invite you to work with me. You can schedule a complimentary consultation to discuss the available options.

https://www.ayurvedichealingcenter.com/on-line-services/free-initial-consultation/

You can also find me under directories/influencers on the KS Media Group App – Apple and Google Play.

Much Love,

Meena Puri

Share the Knowledge

If you enjoyed this book, please leave a review on Amazon. This is how others will find it easily.

You may also email me at mpuri@ayurvedichealingcenter.com I would love to hear from you.

Most importantly, tell your friends, neighbours, family members, and co-workers about it. Almost every single person will benefit from what's shared here.

By the Same Author

"Healing Your Relationship with Food: The Ayurveda Answer"

This book is available on Amazon.

About the Author

Born in India into a family of Ayurvedic Doctors, Meena Puri has a reputation for being wise beyond her years and she very much is carrying the legacy of her late father, Dr. C.R. Puri. She is a compassionate practitioner with highly developed intuitive and listening skills. She is an expert/influencer in her field and is featured in the KS Media Group App.

She lives the teachings and insists on seeing the blessing in her own life's challenges. Meena believes you can heal from anything and holds the same belief for her clients.

She is the founder of The Yoga School of Milford and Ayurvedic Healing Center, Inc. She has a clinical practice in Toronto but works with clients from all over the world. In addition, she leads meditation retreats, group and mentorship programs.

For more information on how Meena can be your guide in your healing journey, visit her website at www.ayruvedichealingcenter.com

If you are ready to take the next step in your healing journey, you may schedule a complimentary consultation with Meena at

www.ayurvedichealingcenter.com/on-line-services/free-initial-consultation/

Made in United States
North Haven, CT
25 March 2022

17556168R00109